Data for Better Governance

This book, along with any associated content or subsequent updates, can be accessed at
https://hdl.handle.net/10986/42413.

Reproducible Research Repository

https://reproducibility.worldbank.org

A reproducibility package is available for this book in
the Reproducible Research Repository at
https://reproducibility.worldbank.org/index.php/catalog/209.

Scan to learn about the
Government Analytics collection.

Data for Better Governance

Building Government Analytics Ecosystems in Latin America and the Caribbean

JUAN FRANCISCO SANTINI,
FLAVIA SACCO CAPURRO,
DANIEL ROGGER, TIMOTHY LUNDY,
GALILEU KIM, JORGE DE LEÓN MIRANDA,
SERENA COCCIOLO, AND CHIARA CASANOVA

© 2024 International Bank for Reconstruction and Development / The World Bank
1818 H Street NW, Washington, DC 20433
Telephone: 202-473-1000; Internet: www.worldbank.org

Some rights reserved

1 2 3 4   27 26 25 24

This work is a product of the staff of The World Bank with external contributions. The findings, interpretations, and conclusions expressed in this work do not necessarily reflect the views of The World Bank, its Board of Executive Directors, or the governments they represent.

The World Bank does not guarantee the accuracy, completeness, or currency of the data included in this work and does not assume responsibility for any errors, omissions, or discrepancies in the information, or liability with respect to the use of or failure to use the information, methods, processes, or conclusions set forth. The boundaries, colors, denominations, links/footnotes, and other information shown in this work do not imply any judgment on the part of The World Bank concerning the legal status of any territory or the endorsement or acceptance of such boundaries. The citation of works authored by others does not mean The World Bank endorses the views expressed by those authors or the content of their works.

Nothing herein shall constitute or be construed or considered to be a limitation upon or waiver of the privileges and immunities of The World Bank, all of which are specifically reserved.

Rights and Permissions

This work is available under the Creative Commons Attribution 3.0 IGO license (CC BY 3.0 IGO) http://creativecommons.org/licenses/by/3.0/igo. Under the Creative Commons Attribution license, you are free to copy, distribute, transmit, and adapt this work, including for commercial purposes, under the following conditions:

Attribution—Please cite the work as follows: Santini, Juan Francisco, Flavia Sacco Capurro, Daniel Rogger, Timothy Lundy, Galileu Kim, Jorge de León Miranda, Serena Cocciolo, and Chiara Casanova. 2024. *Data for Better Governance: Building Government Analytics Ecosystems in Latin America and the Caribbean*. Washington, DC: World Bank. doi:10.1596/978-1-4648-2159-2. License: Creative Commons Attribution CC BY 3.0 IGO

Translations—If you create a translation of this work, please add the following disclaimer along with the attribution: *This translation was not created by The World Bank and should not be considered an official World Bank translation. The World Bank shall not be liable for any content or error in this translation.*

Adaptations—If you create an adaptation of this work, please add the following disclaimer along with the attribution: *This is an adaptation of an original work by The World Bank. Views and opinions expressed in the adaptation are the sole responsibility of the author or authors of the adaptation and are not endorsed by The World Bank.*

Third-party content—The World Bank does not necessarily own each component of the content contained within the work. The World Bank therefore does not warrant that the use of any third-party-owned individual component or part contained in the work will not infringe on the rights of those third parties. The risk of claims resulting from such infringement rests solely with you. If you wish to re-use a component of the work, it is your responsibility to determine whether permission is needed for that re-use and to obtain permission from the copyright owner. Examples of components can include, but are not limited to, tables, figures, or images.

All queries on rights and licenses should be addressed to World Bank Publications, The World Bank, 1818 H Street NW, Washington, DC 20433, USA; e-mail: pubrights@worldbank.org.

ISBN (paper): 978-1-4648-2159-2
ISBN (electronic): 978-1-4648-2178-3
DOI: 10.1596/978-1-4648-2159-2

Cover image: © Pixel Matrix / Adobe Stock. Used with the permission of Pixel Matrix / Adobe Stock. Further permission required for reuse.

Cover design: Bill Pragluski, Critical Stages, LLC.

Library of Congress Control Number: 2024950453

Contents

Foreword ix
Acknowledgments xi
About This Collection xiii
About the Authors xv
Main Messages xvii
Executive Summary xxi
Abbreviations xxv

Chapter 1 The Case for Government Analytics in Latin America and the Caribbean 1

    Introduction 1
    Key Messages 4
    The Government Analytics Ecosystem 5
    Regional Opportunities and Challenges for Government Analytics 6
    A Regional Assessment and Policy Recommendations to Strengthen Government Analytics 10
    Notes 15
    References 16

Chapter 2 A Conceptual Framework for Government Analytics 19

    Introduction 19
    How Does Government Analytics Improve Government Functioning? 21
    What Enabling Conditions Support Government Analytics? 29
    Notes 37
    References 37

Chapter 3 Case Studies of Government Analytics in Latin America and the Caribbean 39

    Introduction 39
    Case Study 3.1: Using Descriptive Analytics to Reduce Missed Medical Appointments (Chile) 40

Case Study 3.2: Using Diagnostic Analytics of Human Resources Data
to Explore the Gender Pay Gap (Colombia) ... 42

Case Study 3.3: Data Analytics for Citizen Accountability—The Case of
reAcción (Paraguay) ... 44

Case Study 3.4: Building an Integrated Human Resources Management
Platform for Strategic Workforce Planning (Uruguay) ... 45

Case Study 3.5: Analyzing Tax Data to Increase Corporate
Tax Collection (Ecuador) ... 47

Case Study 3.6: Using Predictive Analytics to Prevent School
Dropouts (Guatemala) ... 49

Case Study 3.7: Using Tax Data to Boost Procurement Efficiency (Brazil) ... 50

Case Study 3.8: Improving Government Efficiency through a
Centralized Analytics Unit (Colombia) ... 51

Case Study 3.9: Establishing a Decentralized Analytics Unit
to Improve the Efficiency of Tax Collection (Peru) ... 54

Case Study 3.10: Datathons as a Tool for Promoting Data Analytics
(Multiple Countries) ... 55

Case Study 3.11: The Power of Data Integration to Strengthen the
Integrity of Public Procurement (Brazil) ... 56

Case Study 3.12: Supporting the Implementation of Framework
Agreements through Data Analytics (Uruguay) ... 57

Notes ... 58

References ... 59

Chapter 4 A Regional Assessment of Government Analytics in Latin America and the Caribbean ... 61

Introduction ... 61

Survey Methodology ... 63

What Does Government Analytics Look Like in Latin America
and the Caribbean? ... 64

What Analytical Capabilities Do Governments in the Region Possess? ... 70

What Is the State of Data Infrastructure in the Region? ... 74

Notes ... 82

References ... 82

Chapter 5 Policy Recommendations to Strengthen Government Analytics in Latin America and the Caribbean ... 83

Introduction ... 83

Policy Recommendations ... 84

Conclusion ... 89

References ... 90

APPENDIXES

Appendix A	Survey Methodology	91
Appendix B	Types of Management Information Systems and Their Functions	97

BOXES

1.1	*The Government Analytics Handbook*	3
1.2	Why Administrative Data?	8

FIGURES

1.1	Central Government Revenue and Spending Composition in Latin America and the Caribbean, 2010–22	7
1.2	Coverage of Key Management Information Systems in Latin America and the Caribbean and Worldwide	9
2.1	A Conceptual Framework for Government Analytics	20
2.2	Cumulative Fiscal Savings in Three Wage Bill Policy Scenarios, Brazil, 2019–30	23
2.3	Enabling Conditions for Government Analytics	29
3.1	Using Descriptive Analytics to Reduce Missed Medical Appointments, Chile	42
3.2	Building an Integrated Human Resources Management Platform for Strategic Workforce Planning, Uruguay	47
3.3	Using Predictive Analytics to Prevent School Dropouts, Guatemala	50
3.4	Improving Government Efficiency through a Centralized Analytics Unit, Colombia	53
4.1	Types of Analytics, by Type of MIS	64
4.2	Types of Analytics, by Country and Type of MIS	65
4.3	Data Elements Used for Analytics, by Type of MIS	66
4.4	Applications of Analytical Products	68
4.5	Applications of Analytical Products, by Type of MIS	69
4.6	Kinds of Analytical Production, by Type of MIS	70
4.7	Career Tracks for and Training and Assessments on Analytics	71
4.8	Opportunities for Internal Funding and Collaboration with Academics, Nonprofits, or Multilateral Organizations on Analytics Projects, by Type of MIS	72
4.9	Drivers of Collaboration on Analytics with Academics, Nonprofits, or Multilateral Organizations	73

4.10	Fully Digitalized Systems, by Type of MIS	75
4.11	Fully Digitalized Systems, by Country and Type of MIS	75
4.12	Formal Data Access Protocols, by Type of MIS	78
4.13	Formal Data Access Protocols, by Country and Type of MIS	78
4.14	Data Quality Controls in Place, by Type of MIS	80

MAP

| 4.1 | Countries in Latin America and the Caribbean That Participated in the Survey | 62 |

TABLES

1.1	Summary of Case Studies	11
1.2	Key Findings and Policy Recommendations for Strengthening Government Analytics	14
A.1	Countries and Organizations That Participated in the Survey	92
A.2	Countries That Participated in the Survey, by Questionnaire	95

Foreword

Improving the quality of governance is critical to virtually all the agendas in Latin America and the Caribbean (LAC), whether they are providing better and more responsive social services, accelerating growth, ensuring public safety, or supporting lagging areas. Further, high debt service levels and the absence of public fiscal space put a premium on using available resources as efficiently as possible.

The LAC region is well positioned to make progress on these challenges. It has invested heavily over the past 20 years in building information systems to underpin government business. The data stored and tracked in digital management information systems in the region now cover an average of 79 percent of total government revenue and grants and at least 40 percent of the total spending of the central government.

Embedded in every byte of these data is an opportunity to strengthen the quality of the region's governance. Each byte acts not just as a record of government business but also as a diagnostic of its strengths and weaknesses. The repurposing of government administrative data toward strengthening public administration is what the World Bank has termed "government analytics." In line with transformations of private sector companies based on the value inherent in large collections of data, the public sector has an opportunity to change its own production function for better service delivery and more effective government.

This repurposing of government administrative data toward a diagnostic purpose is challenging, and it requires that data systems be made accessible to analysts and that analysts have the capabilities to deliver useful insights from these data. This requires the right staff in the right places, a culture of evidence-based policy making, and national commitment over time.

This report explores the extent to which LAC governments are indeed analyzing their administrative data to strengthen the functioning of public administration. The picture painted is that government analytics is being done in LAC, but its potential remains largely untapped. There is little longer-term strategic vision, training is ad hoc and disparate, and data systems could be coordinated much better.

As the examples provided in *The Government Analytics Handbook* (2023) show, the impact of realizing our regional potential for undertaking government analytics in terms of performance and efficiency is huge, leading to hundreds of millions of dollars in additional government revenue, better personnel management, and immediate improvements in the targeting of resources to schools and more responsive health provision. This volume in the Government Analytics collection provides a road map to realize that potential and a link between academic studies and practical policy measures. We have much to do.

William F. Maloney
Chief Economist, Latin America and the Caribbean Region
Former Chief Economist, Equitable Growth, Finance, and
Institutions Vice Presidency
The World Bank

Acknowledgments

This report is a product of the Bureaucracy Lab, a partnership between the World Bank's Governance Global Practice (GGP) and Development Impact (DECDI) Group. It was produced in collaboration with the GGP—in particular, the Governance Team in the Latin America and the Caribbean Region (LCR); the Public Institutions Data and Analytics Global Unit; and the Public Administration Global Unit. The report is funded by the Office of the Chief Economist for LCR, with the objective of assessing and providing guidance on how to strengthen the use of analytics to governments in the region. It was produced by a core team consisting of Chiara Casanova, Serena Cocciolo, Jorge de León Miranda, Galileu Kim, Timothy Lundy, Daniel Rogger, Flavia Sacco Capurro, and Juan Francisco Santini. We would like to thank a former consultant at the Bureaucracy Lab, Anna Paula Matos, who contributed to this report in its early stages.

The report was produced under the overall guidance of William F. Maloney (chief economist, LCR), Arianna Legovini (director, DECDI), Arturo Herrera (global director, GGP), Oscar Calvo-Gonzalez (regional director, LCR), and Chiara Bronchi (practice manager, GGP Public Institutions Data and Analytics Global Unit). We are grateful to Eric Arias (economist), Elizabeth Grandio (senior procurement specialist), Zahid Hasnain (lead governance specialist), Silvana Kostenbaum (senior public sector specialist), Alberto Leyton (practice manager, GGP), Bernard Myers (senior public sector specialist), Diana Parra Silva (senior public sector specialist), Francesca Recanatini (lead economist), Ruben Ruano Chinchilla (senior public sector specialist), Luciano Wuerzius (senior procurement specialist), and the Governance and Procurement teams in LCR for their overall guidance and support. We thank Cem Dener (lead public sector specialist), Hunt La Cascia (senior public sector specialist), Hubert Nii-Aponsah (consultant), and the GovTech team for their generous guidance in structuring the report and implementing a regional survey on government analytics. We also extend our gratitude to the three reviewers of the report's concept note—Adrian Fozzard (practice manager), Sebastian Galiani (professor, University of Maryland), and Daniel Ortega (lead governance specialist)—for their insightful comments and valuable guidance throughout the writing of this report. We thank the three peer reviewers for the final version of the report—Cem Dener, Julia Michal Clark, and Daniel Ortega—for their helpful comments. Last, we would like to thank Mariano Lafuente, Carlos Pimenta, Alejandro Rasteletti, and David Rivera at the Inter-American Development Bank for sharing their experience developing analytics in Latin America and the Caribbean, as well as Charlotte van Ooijen and Luanna Roncaratti for sharing their expertise on digital government.

Finally, we would like to thank the government officials who were partners in the design and creation of the evidence presented in this report. More than 100 government officials from 20 countries coordinated the completion of the regional survey on government analytics in Latin America and the Caribbean, and their contributions were essential to the completion of the report. In particular, we would like to thank Charlene Laing (The Bahamas), Nicola Callender (Barbados), Maria Pech and Alexia Peralta (Belize), Khantuta Muruchi and Francisco Belmonte (Bolivia), Ciro Avelino and Ronnie Dilli (Brazil), Jose Inostroza and Rafael Hernández (Chile), Manuela Serrano (Colombia), Erick Mora (Costa Rica), Jermaine Jean-Pierre (Dominica), Alejandra Perez and Edwin Rodriguez (Dominican Republic), Juan Yepez (Ecuador), Hugo Forkel and Daniel de León (Guatemala), Heidy Alachán (Honduras), Gary Campbell and Anika Shurrleworth (Jamaica), Evelyn Rodriguez (Panama), Laura Salinas (Paraguay), Darwin Quispe (Peru), Caswallon Duncan (St. Vincent and the Grenadines), Shelley-Ann Clarke and Natasha Ottley (Trinidad and Tobago), and Ignacio Velazco (Uruguay).

About This Collection

This report is part of a World Bank collection examining how analytics using government microdata is revolutionizing public administration throughout the world. The collection is based on *The Government Analytics Handbook* (2023), a comprehensive guide to using data to understand and improve government. The collection encompasses practical guides and resources for policy makers and public officials around the world seeking to improve government functioning by better using their administrative and survey data. It includes *The Government Analytics Handbook* and associated tools as well as region-specific reports, data, and approaches for practitioners seeking a deeper understanding of government analytics.

The general principle of the *Handbook* is as follows: governments across the world make thousands of personnel management decisions, procure millions of goods and services, and execute billions of processes each day. They are data rich. And yet there is little systematic practice to date that capitalizes on these data to make public administrations work better. This means that governments are missing out on data insights to save billions in procurement expenditures, recruit better talent into government, and identify sources of corruption—to name just a few.

The *Handbook* seeks to change that. It presents frontier evidence and practitioner insights on how to leverage data to make governments work better. Covering a range of microdata sources—such as administrative data and public servant surveys—as well as tools and resources for undertaking analytics, it transforms the ability of governments to take a data-informed approach to diagnose and improve how public organizations work.

 Throughout this report, gold callout balloons will be used to point out chapters in *The Government Analytics Handbook* where you can learn more about each topic the report discusses.

About the Authors

Chiara Casanova is a marketing and communications specialist in the World Bank's Development Impact Group. She is an experienced strategic communications professional specializing in social impact and development projects, with a background in public affairs and corporate communications. Her extensive background lies in developing and implementing integrated communication strategies for private, nonprofit, and international development clients. She holds a master's degree in public relations and corporate communications from Georgetown University.

Serena Cocciolo is an economist in the World Bank's Governance Global Practice for the Middle East and North Africa and a member of the Bureaucracy Lab. Her work has focused on strengthening public administrations, public procurement, institutions, and governance. She joined the World Bank after completing her dissertation on community participation in development projects and field applications in the water and education sector. She holds a PhD in economics from Stockholm University.

Jorge de León Miranda is a research and project management professional with more than 10 years of international development work focused on public sector management, public financial management, fiscal policy, macroeconomics, and education. His projects have covered several countries in Latin America and the Caribbean, Africa, the Middle East, and Central Asia. He has also held positions at Ernst and Young, the Inter-American Development Bank, the International Monetary Fund, and the Ministry of Economy of Guatemala. He holds an MA in international economics and finance from the Johns Hopkins University School of Advanced International Studies.

Galileu Kim is a public sector specialist in the Public Institutions Data and Analytics Global Unit in the Governance Global Practice of the World Bank. His work focuses on how governments can leverage data and analytics to improve public administration, with a methodological focus on large-scale administrative data. He is a member of the World Bank's Bureaucracy Lab and a former researcher in the Development Impact Group. He is a research fellow in Brazil's National School of Administration. He holds a PhD in political science from Princeton University.

Timothy Lundy is an editor and writing consultant in the World Bank's Development Impact Group. He holds a PhD in English and comparative literature from Columbia University.

Daniel Rogger is a senior economist in the World Bank's Development Impact Group. He manages the group's Governance and Institution Building unit and is colead of the World Bank's Bureaucracy Lab, a collaboration between the group and the Governance Global Practice that aims to bridge research and policy to strengthen public administration. His research focuses on the organization of the delivery of public goods. He is a cofounder of the Worldwide Bureaucracy Indicators, Global Survey of Public Servants, and Microdata and Evidence for Government Action initiatives. He was a PhD scholar at the Institute for Fiscal Studies, where he is now an international research fellow. He holds a PhD in economics from University College London.

Flavia Sacco Capurro is a data coordinator in the World Bank's Development Impact Group working on issues related to public sector employment and reforms, government analytics, and gender in the public sector. Before joining the group, she was a consultant in the Poverty and Equity Global Practice in the Latin America and the Caribbean Region, working on projects related to poverty analysis, inequality, gender, social development, and fiscal policy. Previously, she worked for the government of Paraguay in the Ministry of Economic and Social Planning. She holds a master's degree in public policy from the University of Chicago.

Juan Francisco Santini is a researcher in the Governance and Institution Building unit of the World Bank's Development Impact Group, a member of the World Bank's Bureaucracy Lab, and a Visiting Research Fellow at Brazil's National School of Public Administration. Before joining the World Bank, he was a Research Fellow at Innovations for Poverty Action and worked for the Inter-American Development Bank, among other institutions. His research and policy interests lie in development economics, particularly its intersection with public economics and public management. He holds a PhD in economics from the Pontifical Catholic University of Rio de Janeiro, Brazil.

Main Messages

Governments in Latin America and the Caribbean face complex development challenges, from slowing economic growth and inflation to persistent institutional weaknesses across the public sector. Strengthening government functioning to respond effectively to these challenges requires a detailed understanding of what is failing and where. It requires diagnostics based on granular, real-time information and the ability for every public servant to take action.

Governments already have the data they need to meet the challenges they face. They have been producing and collecting data in great detail and for many years. But they need to be able to analyze the data they collect in the course of their everyday operations to inform managerial decisions across every government function. For instance, data on recruitment practices can inform human resources management decisions, data on payment delays can improve procurement processes, and data on taxpayer compliance can help design tax instruments. By not taking advantage of the data that are now being collected in digital systems all over the region, governments are leaving substantial amounts of money on the table and diminishing their impact on the lives of citizens.

Data for Better Governance: Building Government Analytics Ecosystems in Latin America and the Caribbean provides a conceptual framework and empirical evidence for evaluating how governments use administrative data to improve the functioning of the state, and it highlights opportunities for improvement. Governments in Latin America and the Caribbean are world leaders in the digitalization of government work—but they do not systematically use the data they have collected to diagnose and improve their functioning. This represents a missed opportunity.

The report offers governments in this region and beyond a road map for *government analytics:* repurposing government data to improve the efficiency and effectiveness of each aspect of government functioning. It identifies the critical enabling conditions for government analytics—data infrastructure and analytical capabilities—and it offers strategies for strengthening them. The report draws on data from a survey of government officials from 20 countries in Latin America and the Caribbean who are experts in core government functions and their respective management information systems, as well as 12 case studies of analytical initiatives, to present the following key findings and recommendations.

EXPANDING THE USE OF GOVERNMENT ANALYTICS IN LATIN AMERICA AND THE CARIBBEAN

The use of analytics in Latin America and the Caribbean varies across government functions and policy areas. There is also significant heterogeneity in the systems and practices used within countries. This suggests that governments lack a systematic approach to analytics for the whole of public administration. This also presents an opportunity for cross-fertilization, allowing countries to share their experiences and adopt successful practices demonstrated by their peers.

Governments in the region can use advanced analytics more extensively to address complex development challenges. Governments predominantly use administrative data to produce descriptive analytics for operational and transactional purposes, but they miss out on opportunities to use advanced analytics to improve decision-making, design more effective and efficient public policies, and strengthen public sector functioning and service delivery.

The impact of government analytics is already being felt in the region. For example, Ecuador and Peru have collected millions of dollars in additional tax revenue by analyzing transactional and external data to detect evasion and better allocate resources for enforcement. Guatemala has improved education services by analyzing student-level data to identify and support at-risk students, reducing dropout rates by 9 percent for students at a pivotal moment in their education. These examples demonstrate that governments can use analytics to improve many different aspects of their operations, capitalizing on the wealth of data contained in their management information systems.

BUILDING ENABLING CONDITIONS FOR GOVERNMENT ANALYTICS

Governments must complete the digitalization of their management information systems. Two-thirds of the experts surveyed reported that their systems are not fully digitalized. Levels of digitalization vary substantially by government function: information systems for taxation and public financial management exhibit a relatively high degree of digitalization, while health management information systems have the lowest degree of digitalization. Incomplete digitalization results in data infrastructure problems that prevent governments from fully leveraging their administrative data to improve policy design and implementation.

High-quality, integrated data are essential to analytics, but data fragmentation and isolated information systems constrain digitalization. Outdated or inadequate data infrastructure limits the quality and accessibility of administrative data, making it difficult for organizations to use these data for analytics and policy making. When management information systems are fragmented, various subsystems operate independently, making it virtually impossible to create a centralized, fully digitalized system. Consequently, data sharing and interoperability between the different systems are restricted, the quality of data available for analytics is compromised, and the available data do not always align with strategic priorities and policy needs.

Information systems need mechanisms to ensure the quality of the data they contain. According to the World Bank's GovTech Maturity Index, only 25 percent of countries in Latin America and the Caribbean have implemented a data quality framework, which is lower than the implementation rate in other regions. When data quality controls are not integrated into an information system, each team using the system's data must conduct its own quality control process, resulting in inefficiencies. Moreover, the lack of systematic controls can undermine the accuracy, reliability, and replicability of analytics.

Improving data accessibility and system interoperability should be a government-wide effort. According to the GovTech Maturity Index, less than 35 percent of countries in Latin America and the Caribbean have implemented a government interoperability framework that allows for efficient and secure information exchange between government systems and organizations. Sharing information enables new and innovative analytical applications: Brazil has repurposed tax data to boost procurement efficiency, reducing purchase prices by about 13 percent. If governments establish the foundational infrastructure for interoperability, they can advance their overall potential for using data for analytics and policy making enormously.

Data systems are not enough; public administration must change, too. **Governments can systematize the use of analytics in decision-making by incorporating dedicated analytics units into the organizational structure of public administration.** In Colombia, for instance, a dedicated analytics unit has supported quality-of-life improvements, information sharing, and public service delivery for the entire city of Bogotá, thanks to its centralized organizational model. On the other hand, relying on part-time teams for analytical tasks can lead to suboptimal outcomes because these teams might prioritize immediate operational needs over broader analytical objectives.

INTEGRATING DATA ANALYTICS INTO DECISION-MAKING PROCESSES

Analytics is a tool, not a replacement for decision-makers or experience. Analytics cannot replace decision-makers, design policies, or substitute for the experience and knowledge of policy makers and public servants. But officials must be given the ability to use the evidence provided by analytics to guide key decisions, identify gaps and weaknesses, and refine the design and implementation of policy interventions. Training to support decision-makers and data analysts in using government analytics is fragmented and weak across Latin America and the Caribbean. This can be improved rapidly.

Governments in the region need more structured efforts to attract and retain skilled data analysts at all levels of seniority. Offering career tracks for data analysts is critical to building a robust government analytics ecosystem. Governments in the region face a shortage of structured career development opportunities in analytics: only 12 percent of governments have a dedicated career track for data analysts.

Finally, governments must foster a culture of evidence-based decision-making, which is essential to using government analytics to transform public administration. Analytics is more impactful when policy makers ask for the evidence they need and use it to shape policies and inform critical decisions. The region's governments require a deeper culture of evidence-based decision-making. Knowledge exchange on best practices and successful experiences can increase decision-makers' awareness of the benefits of grounding policy decisions in data and evidence. Improving decision-makers' knowledge and ability to comprehend data analytics results—and identify their limitations—is crucial for effectively integrating analytical findings into decision-making processes.

Latin America and the Caribbean—and the rest of the world—has the data it needs to improve government. Now is the time to use them.

Executive Summary

INTRODUCTION

Governments in Latin America and the Caribbean face complex development challenges. The region is at substantial risk from slowing economic growth, inflation, and fiscal pressures, and its public sector is constrained by institutional weaknesses, including inefficient public spending and service delivery. Core functions of government, including human resources management and public financial management, require substantial improvements in their efficiency and effectiveness. Strengthening government functioning requires actionable diagnostics, based on granular, real-time information: for instance, data on recruitment practices to inform human resources management decisions, data on payment delays to improve procurement processes, and data on taxpayer compliance to design tax instruments. Governments can use administrative data that are specific to government functions to inform managerial decisions to improve those functions.

Governments in Latin America and the Caribbean are well positioned to leverage data for better government. The region is a global pioneer in establishing management information systems (MISs): specialized systems that collect administrative data on specific functions of government, including human resources, procurement, service delivery, taxes, and more. These information systems gather granular, real-time data on core government functions, and these data can serve as a rich source of information on challenges and opportunities in these functions. However, the administrative data recorded in these information systems are often underutilized because of inadequate data quality and accessibility, as well as limited analytical capabilities within governments. By addressing these constraints, governments can use administrative data to improve the efficiency and effectiveness of each aspect of government functioning.

A reproducibility package is available for this book in the Reproducible Research Repository at https://reproducibility.worldbank.org/index.php/catalog/209.

THIS REPORT

This report outlines how governments in Latin America and the Caribbean can enable the use of their administrative data to strengthen government functioning, a practice the report refers to as *government analytics*. It provides a conceptual framework that governments can use to assess how they employ administrative data for analytics and identify areas for improvement. The framework can be applied to different information systems and their corresponding functions (for instance, education and health services, procurement, and taxation), and it provides detailed insights and recommendations to improve the use of data for each core function. For example, a government may be using its tax data to their full analytical potential while underutilizing human resources data for personnel management.

The report argues that governments can better leverage their data to improve their functioning by focusing on the enabling conditions for analytics: data infrastructure and analytical capabilities. For each type of information system, governments should build data infrastructure that ensures data are accurate, high-coverage, and accessible. As a whole, governments can strengthen their analytical capabilities by setting up dedicated analytical units and career tracks for data analysts. Government analytics and its enabling conditions are part of an ecosystem: by improving the enabling conditions for analytics, governments create an environment in which administrative data can be used to strengthen their functioning, improving effectiveness and efficiency in human resources management, procurement, taxation, and more.

Guided by the conceptual framework, the report provides evidence on the government analytics landscape in Latin America and the Caribbean. First, it presents 12 case studies documenting how governments in the region have leveraged their administrative data to improve specific aspects of government functioning. These case studies cover a wide set of countries, information systems, and government functions, highlighting the significant value and impact of government analytics. For instance, Ecuador and Peru have collected millions of dollars in additional tax revenue by analyzing tax data to detect evasion and better allocate resources for enforcement. Guatemala has improved education services, reducing student dropout rates by analyzing education data to identify and support at-risk students. The case studies illustrate that governments can use analytics to enhance distinct dimensions of their functioning, drawing on the richness of administrative data.

Next, the report presents quantitative data from an original survey of government officials conducted in 20 countries and across six types of information systems, offering the first comprehensive picture of government analytics and its enabling conditions in Latin America and the Caribbean. In each country, the survey questionnaires were answered by public servants from institutions responsible for managing different information systems. The respondents assessed the extent to which institutions in core functions of government use administrative data to improve their functioning. The regional survey reveals significant variation in the use of government analytics, the state of data infrastructure, and the strength of analytical capabilities across different governments and their core functions.

Governments in Latin America and the Caribbean predominantly use descriptive analytics. Their use of diagnostic and predictive analytics is uneven and is mostly concentrated on taxation and service delivery. They do not substantially use diagnostic and predictive analytics for cross-cutting government functions, such as human resources management, procurement, and public financial management. In sum, governments in the region primarily use analytics to strengthen the revenue side of their operations (for instance, taxation) rather than the expenditure side (for instance, procurement). Across information systems, governments primarily apply analytics for monitoring, with less focus on policy evaluation and design. This means that governments underutilize their administrative data for more complex types of analytics that could help them diagnose and address the causes of inefficiencies. By expanding the use of different types of analytics for all their functions, governments can enhance the efficiency and effectiveness of public administration more broadly.

The survey also reveals opportunities for institutional reform. Some information systems in the region are only partially digitalized, limiting the quality and comprehensiveness of the administrative data they generate. For example, health information systems are rarely fully digitalized, owing to the use of paper records. Information systems also exhibit significant gaps in data governance. In education, health, and public financial management, data accessibility is restricted by a lack of formalized access protocols. In addition, whereas data quality controls are widespread for education and tax systems, procurement, public financial management, and health information systems lag behind. Interoperability among information systems and data sharing among government organizations are similarly limited. The survey also underscores the challenges governments face in developing their analytical capabilities. Many lack structured career tracks for data analysts, targeted training in analytical skills, and adequate funding for analytical projects. These constraints limit governments' capacity to expand the use of data to improve their functioning.

Finally, based on the survey and case studies and guided by the conceptual framework, the report presents a set of policy recommendations. First, governments should identify evidence gaps for policy making and create awareness of how administrative data could help fill these gaps, boosting demand for government analytics. They should aim to strengthen their use of descriptive analytics and move toward diagnostic and predictive analytics applications to inform policy evaluation and design. Governments should also invest further in the enabling conditions for government analytics. To build analytical capabilities, governments should develop targeted data analytics training programs and set up institutional pathways for applying analytical skills. This can be done by establishing career tracks for analysts, setting up dedicated analytics units, allocating a stable budget for training and analytical products, and fostering collaborations with academic partners. To strengthen data infrastructure, governments should institute systematic data quality controls, develop comprehensive and accessible data inventories, enhance data connectivity and information system interoperability, and establish protocols for maintaining and updating their e-government systems.

This report is part of a series of World Bank publications focusing on government analytics, including *The Government Analytics Handbook* (Rogger and Schuster 2023). It is designed as a guide for policy makers and senior public officials who want to improve government functioning by using their administrative data to its full potential. As such, the report does not extensively cover the technical details of implementation, but it provides additional references for practitioners seeking a deeper understanding of the technical requirements for government analytics. By using this report's conceptual framework and survey as a starting point, governments can assess their use of government analytics and assign priority levels to actions to build a more efficient and effective public administration.

REFERENCE

Rogger, Daniel, and Christian Schuster, eds. 2023. *The Government Analytics Handbook: Leveraging Data to Strengthen Public Administration*. Washington, DC: World Bank. https://doi.org/10.1596/978-1-4648-1957-5.

Abbreviations

COVID-19	coronavirus disease 2019
CV	curriculum vitae
DECDI	Development Impact Group [World Bank organizational unit]
DNCP	Dirección Nacional de Contrataciones Públicas (National Public Procurement Agency) [Paraguay]
EdMIS	education management information system
ENTRE	Estrategia Nacional para la Transición Exitosa (National Strategy for Successful Transition) [Guatemala]
FONACIDE	Fondo Nacional de Inversión Pública y Desarrollo (National Public Investment and Development Fund) [Paraguay]
GDP	gross domestic product
GGP	Governance Global Practice [World Bank organizational unit]
GRAS	Governance Risk Assessment System
HealthMIS	health management information system
HRMIS	human resources management information system
LCR	Latin America and the Caribbean Region [World Bank operational unit]
MINEDUC	Ministerio de Educación (Ministry of Education) [Guatemala]
MINSAL	Ministerio de Salud (Ministry of Health) [Chile]
MIS	management information system
NSO	national statistical office
ONSC	Oficina Nacional del Servicio Civil (National Civil Service Office) [Uruguay]
PFMIS	public financial management information system
SEFAZ/RS	Secretaria da Fazenda do Estado do Rio Grande do Sul (Secretariat of Finance of the State of Rio Grande do Sul) [Brazil]
SRI	Servicio de Rentas Internas (Internal Revenue Service) [Ecuador]

SUNAT	Superintendencia Nacional de Aduanas y de Administración Tributaria (National Superintendency of Customs and Tax Administration) [Peru]
TaxMIS	tax management information system
UCD	Unidad de Científicos de Datos (Data Scientists Unit) [Colombia]
VAT	value added tax

All dollar amounts are US dollars unless otherwise specified.

CHAPTER 1

The Case for Government Analytics in Latin America and the Caribbean

INTRODUCTION

Countries in Latin America and the Caribbean face challenges on several fronts, demanding more efficient and responsive governments that engender confidence among their citizens.

Governments in the region are constrained in making necessary investments as a result of increased deficits and debt arising from the COVID-19 pandemic, pointing to the need for these governments to become more effective and efficient (IMF 2021; Maloney et al. 2024). They have already demonstrated that they can achieve this: for example, relative to 30 years ago, increases in the professionalization and efficiency of ministries of finance and central banks have burnished the region's global reputation for macroeconomic stability. Other core functions of government need to follow. Estimates point to waste of about 4 percent of GDP, or 17 percent of all public spending, on account of inadequate procurement practices, misdirected transfers, and poorly designed human resources management (Izquierdo, Pessino, and Vuletin 2018; World Bank 2022b). In some countries in the region, the estimated waste is even higher.

Recent social unrest in the region also reveals deep popular dissatisfaction with state performance, in areas ranging from pensions to education to antipoverty policies. Citizens' distrust in the government and public institutions, as well as their perceptions of embedded corruption in the state, make them reluctant to vote in favor of large infrastructure projects or contribute with taxes. Doubts about what government institutions offer lead many small entrepreneurs to remain unregistered and informal. Citizens in Latin America and the Caribbean don't just

---

A reproducibility package is available for this book in the Reproducible Research Repository at https://reproducibility.worldbank.org/index.php/catalog/209.

have low "tax morale": they have low faith in governance in general (Keefer and Scartascini 2022).

These demands for effective governance will only become more acute. To adapt to climate change and take advantage of opportunities offered by the green transition and the realignment of the global economy after the COVID-19 pandemic, governments must be able to mobilize more resources, plan strategically, and implement plans efficiently. Demands for a more activist state—one that stimulates innovation and midwifes structural change—have arisen after the disappointing growth rates of the last two decades, which have called into question the tenets of the neoliberal growth model (refer, for example, to Hausmann and Rodrik 2006; Mazzucato and Rodrik 2023). However, many countries have moved to minimize state intervention in the economy, given its poor track record in conceiving and implementing industrial policies in previous decades. Without improvements in state capacity, monitoring, and transparency, governments that engage in a new round of experimental policies will only wind up disappointed again.

It is therefore paramount that governments in Latin America and the Caribbean improve their core functions, including human resources management, procurement, taxation, public financial management, and more. Broad-based improvements in government functioning are fundamental to improving the region's development prospects and must be at the top of national policy agendas. To provide policy tools and support for these agendas, the World Bank produced *The Government Analytics Handbook* (Rogger and Schuster 2023), which consolidates cutting-edge academic and policy evidence on using data analytics to measure government performance and on designing policies to improve it (box 1.1). One lesson from the *Handbook* is that although progress in some areas will remain challenging, there are also relatively quick wins. For instance, improving the performance of the worst-performing procurement officers could reduce a government's annual procurement expenditures by 12 percent (Best, Hjort, and Szakonyi 2023).

This report aims to provide a road map so governments in Latin America and the Caribbean can bring these tools to the front line of policy and use them to enhance their functioning. Governments in the region are well placed to use data to improve their core functions, owing to successive investments in technologies that are foundational for analytics. The region is a global pioneer in establishing management information systems (MISs), which record and store large amounts of data on specific aspects of government functioning—such as taxation, public finance, and human resources management—and make them available. These administrative data are large reservoirs of underutilized evidence and information. By analyzing these data, governments can assess the effectiveness and efficiency of public administration and understand where it can be strengthened. However, because of weaknesses in their analog complements (for instance, data analysts and data access protocols), these data are rarely used for evidence-based policy making (World Bank 2016, 2023). This means governments in Latin America and the Caribbean can do much more with the data they already have to improve their functioning, address development challenges, and build citizens' trust.

Box 1.1 *The Government Analytics Handbook*

This report builds on *The Government Analytics Handbook* (Rogger and Schuster 2023), a comprehensive guide to using government data to strengthen public administration. Governments across the world make thousands of personnel management decisions, procure millions of goods and services, and execute billions of processes each day. When these functions are recorded in management information systems, governments are data rich. Yet there is limited systematic use of the resulting data to strengthen public administration. This means that governments are missing out on opportunities to save money on procurement expenditures, recruit better talent into government, and identify sources of corruption.

The *Handbook* provides comprehensive and in-depth guidance to help governments develop a data-informed approach to government analytics. It brings together evidence and insights from various countries and practitioners into a one-of-a-kind resource covering a range of topics, including survey design, the strategic use of human resources management data, and ethical considerations for data use. It also considers a variety of data sources, including different types of administrative and survey data. In this way, the *Handbook* presents frontier evidence and practitioner insights on how to leverage data to make governments work better.

This report applies lessons from the *Handbook* to Latin America and the Caribbean and draws on relevant examples from the region to help policy makers and senior public officials use government analytics to enhance the effectiveness and efficiency of their public administrations. It focuses on administrative data, because these data are accessible at low cost to most government organizations (refer to box 1.2).

Many governments in the region are already capitalizing on the opportunity to use administrative data to inform policy making. For example, the government in one Brazilian state has reduced procurement prices by 13 percent by using tax data to calculate market reference prices for procurement agents. Chile has saved hundreds of millions of dollars by using health data to design a program to reduce missed medical appointments and improve health behaviors among patients with chronic conditions, and Colombia has saved the lives of thousands of newborns and expectant mothers by tracking health risks. Ecuador and Peru have collected millions of dollars in additional tax revenue by using tax data to detect evasion and better allocate resources for enforcement. And Guatemala has reduced the dropout rate for students entering lower secondary school by 9 percent by using education data to identify and support at-risk students. Through these analytical initiatives, governments have drawn on administrative data they already have to enhance policy design, strengthen service delivery, and reduce inefficiency and waste.[1] This report aims to support initiatives like these by offering guidance on how to build and sustain a robust government analytics ecosystem that facilitates the use of data to improve the functioning of public administration.

KEY MESSAGES

The first key message of this report is that governments in Latin America and the Caribbean can enhance the design and implementation of public policy by using government analytics more broadly and intensively than they currently do. Governments' use of administrative data for analytics varies across different functions and policy areas. The report shows that the revenue side of government operations often makes more extensive use of data to inform its actions. For instance, governments in the region often use advanced analytics of tax data to improve tax compliance. On the expenditure side, however—such as in human resources management and procurement—there is significant room for growth. For instance, governments in the region rely primarily on descriptive analytics of personnel headcount to manage public employees, and they rarely use advanced analytics to forecast public administration's wage bill or to improve the efficiency of public procurement and secure competitive prices. Likewise, there are significant opportunities to develop the use of advanced analytics for service delivery—for example, to forecast student enrollment.

The second key message is that governments must foster two essential enabling conditions to make their administrative data useful for policy making. The first is high-quality, accessible, and integrated data infrastructure. Improving data quality controls and accessibility should be a government-wide effort, enabling economies of scale. Likewise, ensuring that different information systems across the government are interoperable and connecting their data can multiply the potential insights and applications of government analytics. The second is analytical capabilities, such as funding opportunities, dedicated analytical units, and career tracks for data analysts. Government-wide strategies and institutionalized funding streams enable a more harmonized, cohesive approach to developing analytical initiatives, which can facilitate cross-pollination, learning, and collaboration across government organizations.

The final key message is that governments must integrate data analytics into their decision-making processes to use it effectively for policy making and reform. Government analytics is not a solution in itself: it is a tool to provide policy makers with accurate and relevant evidence to guide key decisions, identify gaps and weaknesses, and refine the design and implementation of policy interventions (Rogger and Schuster 2023; World Bank 2021). Analytics cannot replace decision-makers, design policies, or substitute for the experience and knowledge of policy makers and public servants. To be useful, analytics must be problem oriented, demand driven, and responsive to the specific needs of decision-makers, because strengthening the public sector requires more than data and measurement (Bridges and Woolcock 2023). In addition to creating the enabling conditions for analytics, governments must foster a culture of evidence-based decision-making within public administration to ensure that analytics delivers on its potential to enhance the design and implementation of public policy.

 Throughout this report, gold callout balloons will be used to point out chapters in *The Government Analytics Handbook* where you can learn more about each topic the report discusses.

THE GOVERNMENT ANALYTICS ECOSYSTEM

Government analytics can help make public administration more efficient by meeting the needs and objectives of policy makers and informing specific policies and critical decisions. Governments can use data to support evidence-based decision-making in three major ways, as outlined in the World Bank's *World Development Report 2021: Data for Better Lives* (World Bank 2021). First, they can analyze data to improve policy making and service delivery by increasing access to government services and ensuring that policies are grounded in the best available evidence. Second, they can use data to help allocate scarce resources through targeting and monitoring. Finally, they can publicize data to foster transparency and increase their own accountability for using public resources effectively and efficiently (World Bank 2021). Government analytics thus aligns with a broader World Bank agenda on the use of data and analytics to promote development.[2]

Chapter 2 of this report presents a conceptual framework that highlights the different uses of government analytics and how to strengthen its enabling conditions. As the World Bank's *World Development Report 2016: Digital Dividends* (World Bank 2016) highlights, digital technologies require analog complements to achieve their potential. Similarly, analytics requires two essential enabling conditions to be an effective policy-making tool: the infrastructure to produce and use high-quality data and the analytical capabilities to leverage these data. This report uses the metaphor of an *ecosystem* to refer to the interdependence of government analytics applications and their enabling conditions. Just as diverse organisms require an environment that supports them, government analytics is enabled by robust data infrastructure and analytical capabilities.

The conceptual framework first considers how government analytics provides evidence to address policy-making challenges and meet decision-makers' needs. Governments face a wide variety of policy-making challenges that demand diverse evidence and thus diverse analytical products. There are many types of analytical products, each one drawing on different types of administrative data to respond to different policy needs. There can be analytics on taxation or procurement, on human resources or public debt data. For this reason, the conceptual framework describes in detail the different types of analytics governments undertake, how the insights generated by analytics are applied, and how analytics is produced and distributed among public servants and citizens.

Even within a single government function, different challenges might demand different types of analytics. For instance, a government struggling with procurement delays might analyze procurement data to understand the extent of these delays and what causes them. On the other hand, a government considering establishing a centralized payment system might analyze procurement data to predict the effects of the new system. Public administration faces a diverse set of challenges, so the solutions that government analytics provides to policy makers should be diverse as well.

The conceptual framework then describes two enabling conditions that help government analytics yield solutions to policy-making challenges. The first is data infrastructure. Government analytics depends on high-quality data supported by robust data governance and access protocols to ensure they are secure, accurate, and widely used. If the quality of data infrastructure deteriorates, so do the quality and diversity of analytics. The second is analytical capabilities, at both the individual and organizational levels: dedicated career tracks and training for data analysts, funding opportunities, dedicated analytics units, and a comprehensive analytics strategy. These enabling conditions strengthen each other: improvements to data infrastructure provide incentives for investments in analytical capabilities by making administrative data more accessible and easier to use, and stronger analytical capabilities provide incentives for investments in improving data infrastructure, because staff and resources are available to use those data for analytics. Furthermore, analytical applications can help strengthen these enabling conditions: for example, by identifying data gaps and motivating public servants to develop their skills through training.

The conceptual framework also structures the analysis of qualitative and quantitative evidence on government analytics—along with the policy recommendations derived from this evidence—presented in the rest of the report. Chapter 3 presents 12 case studies of analytical initiatives from across Latin America and the Caribbean, covering a wide range of countries and government functions. Then, chapter 4 presents the results of an original survey administered in 20 countries to public servants who are experts in digital government, administrative data, and analytics. Finally, chapter 5 concludes with policy recommendations to help governments at all levels of analytics maturity apply the conceptual framework to develop government analytics and meet the policy-making challenges they face.

REGIONAL OPPORTUNITIES AND CHALLENGES FOR GOVERNMENT ANALYTICS

Governments in Latin America and the Caribbean are well positioned to develop a government analytics ecosystem to support evidence-based policy making and improve their functioning. Countries in the region have invested significant resources in building MISs: integrated data frameworks that collect, store, and manage administrative data across government functions (World Bank 2022a). This report focuses on six MISs that are key to government functioning:

- Human resources management information system (HRMIS)
- Procurement management information system (e-Procurement)
- Public financial management information system (PFMIS)
- Tax management information system (TaxMIS)
- Education management information system (EdMIS)
- Health management information system (HealthMIS).

Together, these MISs cover government functions that account for an average of 79 percent of total revenue and grants and at least 40 percent of total spending at the central government level in Latin America and the Caribbean (figure 1.1). This makes them a vital source of data for governments.[3] (Box 1.2 explains why this report focuses on administrative data, and appendix B describes each MIS in more detail.)

Since the 1980s, governments in Latin America and the Caribbean have made substantial progress in implementing information systems to digitalize, automate, and simplify core government functions. These investments have significantly expanded the availability of digital administrative data across the essential government functions considered in this report (panel a of figure 1.2).[4] By 2022, every country in the region had both a PFMIS and a TaxMIS. Additionally, 91 percent of the countries had an HRMIS, and 84 percent had an e-Procurement system (World Bank 2022a). The extensive adoption of digital MISs makes the region a global leader in information system coverage (panel b of figure 1.2).

FIGURE 1.1 Central Government Revenue and Spending Composition in Latin America and the Caribbean, 2010–22

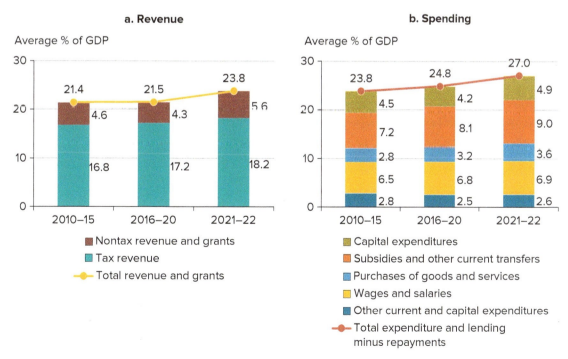

Source: Original figure for this publication, based on data from CEPALSTAT (https://statistics.cepal.org/portal/cepalstat/index.html?lang=en).

Box 1.2   Why Administrative Data?

This report focuses on government analytics using administrative data: information routinely collected and stored by government organizations in management information systems to facilitate program administration and public service delivery. For instance, administrative data include government records of births and deaths, student enrollment, procurement contract values, tax revenues, and the wages of the workforce, among many other records of how public administration translates policy into practice each day.

Administrative data typically offer more frequent and more geographically comprehensive insights into individuals and organizations than are possible with survey data. Because administrative data are collected for administrative purposes, these data are also often less costly than other types of data (Statistics Canada, n.d.; UK Office for Statistics Regulation, n.d.; US Census Bureau, n.d.). Repurposing administrative data for analytics turns them into a valuable resource for improving the design, implementation, management, and assessment of programs, thereby improving government functioning.

Administrative data can also be enhanced and complemented by survey data, which can offer insights into challenges not captured by routinely collected data. However, unlike administrative data, survey data are not readily available to government agencies. This report focuses on government analytics using administrative data, because these data are a powerful but underutilized resource and are accessible to most government organizations.

Administrative data can also improve the operations of government organizations involved in survey data collection, such as national statistical offices (NSOs), creating valuable synergies for the public sector (Rivas and Crowley 2018). Using administrative data from sectors such as tax, health, and education, NSOs can significantly improve the compilation and accuracy of important national statistics. Tax data can support the creation of indexes of economic activity. Similarly, health and education records can be used to verify expenditure data.

NSOs' expertise in data management and governance can likewise add substantial value to administrative data. NSOs can assist in improving data quality through quality controls and ensuring data standardization across the public sector, which in turn facilitates interoperability between data systems. Collaborations between organizations responsible for administrative data and those responsible for survey data thus have great potential to enhance information quality and strengthen government analytics.

The transition from analog to digital MISs creates an opportunity for governments in Latin America and the Caribbean to leverage existing administrative data to improve policy design and implementation. Digital MISs generate an unprecedented amount of data about how public administration works, facilitating measurement at a granular level and in real time. Governments in the region have also built international networks to support the development and scale-up of analytical solutions, such as the Inter-American Network of Digital Government. Investments in government technology, like citizen portals and open data, have strengthened core government systems in the region, enabling the region to make significant progress toward a more data-driven public sector (World Bank 2023).

Despite high MIS coverage, governments in Latin America and the Caribbean must address institutional constraints to fully leverage their administrative data for government analytics. Governments in the region still contend with partial digitalization and fragmentation of their MISs and poor data governance. The challenges of implementing MIS reforms have resulted in a mixture of tools and technologies with varying degrees of effectiveness, leading in turn to information silos and inconsistent data standards. As a result, interoperability among different systems is limited, the quality of data available for analytics is compromised, and the available data do not necessarily align with strategic priorities and policy needs. Governments also face challenges in recruiting and retaining the skilled analysts needed to analyze data and produce useful analytical applications.

FIGURE 1.2 Coverage of Key Management Information Systems in Latin America and the Caribbean and Worldwide

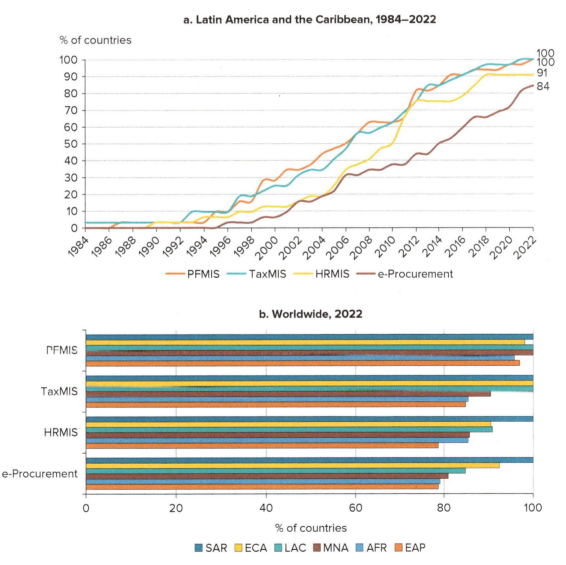

Source: World Bank 2022a.
Note: AFR = Africa; EAP = East Asia and Pacific; ECA = Europe and Central Asia; e-Procurement = procurement management information system; HRMIS = human resources management information system; LAC = Latin America and the Caribbean; MNA = Middle East and North Africa; PFMIS = public financial management information system; SAR = South Asia; TaxMIS = tax management information system.

A REGIONAL ASSESSMENT AND POLICY RECOMMENDATIONS TO STRENGTHEN GOVERNMENT ANALYTICS

This report presents evidence and practical guidance for governments in Latin America and the Caribbean on using their administrative data to improve government functioning. Chapter 3 offers a series of qualitative case studies that provide firsthand accounts of the opportunities and challenges governments in the region have encountered while repurposing administrative data to solve governance challenges through analytics, and the results they have achieved. Table 1.1 summarizes each case study. Then, chapter 4 presents quantitative evidence from an original survey conducted in 20 countries in the region. Public servants in each country who are experts in specific information systems and core government functions responded to questionnaires on the country's government analytics ecosystem. By presenting a variety of analytical experiences in the case studies and survey, this report can help public servants learn from one another's challenges and success stories.

But this report is more than an assessment: it is a practical guide for governments that want to make data analytics a larger part of their policy-making tool kit. Just as a gardening guide explains what environment various plants need to thrive, this report offers recommendations for creating a resilient ecosystem to support diverse analytics applications that can meet a wide variety of policy-making needs. Chapter 5 offers a set of policy recommendations targeting each element of the conceptual framework, based on the findings in the regional assessment. The recommendations are tailored to different levels of information system and analytics maturity so that all governments can find practical next steps for developing analytics for evidence-based policy making. Table 1.2 summarizes these key findings and policy recommendations.

To put these recommendations into practice, governments must be aware of broader political economy challenges. The political context that shapes policy making and the prevailing culture within public administration have a significant impact on the extent to which policies and decisions are informed by evidence. For instance, leaders in public administration may view the accountability promoted by data analytics with discomfort, perceiving it as a threat to their autonomy. Leaders may also make their personal agendas a priority, especially in environments in which electoral competition does not provide incentives for evidence-based policy change. Even when leaders want to make evidence-based policy decisions, the political process might demand quick decisions, without adequate time to gather data, conduct analytics, and produce evidence. Government analytics alone cannot address these constraints.

Using government analytics to improve government functioning, address development challenges, and ultimately build citizens' trust thus requires going beyond the enabling conditions outlined in this report. It also demands continuous support from policy makers and a cultural shift toward embracing evidence-based policy making. This report aims to guide policy makers interested in analytics by offering practical guidance on how to support it institutionally, as well as concrete examples of analytical applications that have successfully enhanced policy design and implementation. The hope is that it offers evidence and inspiration to public servants and policy makers who want to use data to make government work better—in their own countries and for Latin America and the Caribbean as a whole.

TABLE 1.1 Summary of Case Studies

Country	Case study	Summary
Chile	3.1: Using Descriptive Analytics to Reduce Missed Medical Appointments	The Ministry of Health of Chile analyzed HealthMIS data to understand which patients were missing medical appointments—at a cost of $180 million annually—and to design a program to reduce missed appointments and increase primary care use. Implementing a reminder system and remedying gaps in administrative records decreased missed appointments by 6 percent and increased the use of primary care services by about 10 percent among patients with diabetes and hypertension. This case study demonstrates the impact relatively simple descriptive analytics can have when it is based on rich, comprehensive data, as well as the importance of data quality and how analytical projects can help implement quality controls and improve administrative records.
Colombia	3.2: Using Diagnostic Analytics of Human Resources Data to Explore the Gender Pay Gap	The Data Scientists Unit of the National Planning Department of Colombia analyzed HRMIS data to study the question of whether there is a gender pay gap among some public sector workers. It found a gender pay gap of approximately 6 percent and informed the authorities that oversee gender policies of gaps in compliance with Colombia's gender antidiscrimination law. This case study demonstrates that good policy evaluation produces evidence describing not just *what* is happening but also *why* it is happening, as well as the critical role a dedicated analytics unit can play in generating that evidence.
Paraguay	3.3: Data Analytics for Citizen Accountability: The Case of reAcción	Leveraging open procurement data, reAcción Paraguay built an open platform to monitor the allocation of millions of dollars of public funds distributed through a school infrastructure program. The platform's insights prompted a response from the government and improved the targeting of resources to schools with the greatest need by 400 percent. This case study demonstrates how open and accessible government data can empower civic mobilization, enable civil society to uncover mismanagement of public funds, and improve government transparency and accountability and the allocation of public resources. It also demonstrates how the impact of government analytics is amplified when data from different sources are connected.
Uruguay	3.4: Building an Integrated Human Resources Management Platform for Strategic Workforce Planning	The National Civil Service Office of Uruguay is developing a human resources management platform that integrates administrative data from multiple government organizations. The platform will transform public sector recruitment and management and create the enabling conditions for future analytics. This case study demonstrates the impact government analytics can have when data are connected; the powerful applications of descriptive analytics; and the importance of monitoring the composition of the public sector workforce, the skills and competencies within it, and future human capital needs.

(continues on next page)

TABLE 1.1 Summary of Case Studies *(continued)*

Country	Case study	Summary
Ecuador	3.5: Analyzing Tax Data to Increase Corporate Tax Collection	The Internal Revenue Service of Ecuador, in collaboration with a team of researchers, evaluated the integration of third-party data with the country's TaxMIS to combat tax evasion. The evaluation showed that using third-party data in tax collection could generate hundreds of millions of dollars in revenue if complemented by effective enforcement. This case study demonstrates how administrative data can be used for rigorous policy evaluation, the impact of connecting multiple administrative records and nonadministrative databases, and the benefits for public administration of partnerships with external researchers and data analysts.
Guatemala	3.6: Using Predictive Analytics to Prevent School Dropouts	In Guatemala, approximately 40 percent of sixth graders drop out of school before reaching ninth grade. To tackle this issue, the Ministry of Education, in collaboration with the World Bank, piloted an early warning system to identify students at risk of dropping out that leveraged predictive analytics based on recent improvements to student-level data. This innovative program achieved a 9 percent decrease in the dropout rate during the transition from primary to lower secondary school. This case study demonstrates how analytics can support policy evaluation and design and test the effectiveness of policies before scale-up, as well as the importance of high-quality data to enable analytics to have an impact.
Brazil	3.7: Using Tax Data to Boost Procurement Efficiency	The government of the state of Rio Grande do Sul in Brazil used tax data to enhance the efficiency of procurement processes, saving 4 percent on its annual total expenditure for specific products. Since 2008, Brazil has required registered firms that are subject to state tax on the circulation of goods and services to issue digital invoices for their transactions. These data were used to calculate market reference prices for setting tendering parameters. When procurement teams had access to these analytics, purchase prices were reduced by 13.2 percent. This case study shows how government data can be used for analytics across functions and how simple statistics, such as the calculation of reference prices, can be leveraged to improve procurement.
Colombia	3.8: Improving Government Efficiency through a Centralized Analytics Unit	The municipal government of Bogotá, Colombia, created a centralized analytics unit, Ágata, to generate insights across management information systems and government functions to meet the needs of the city's stakeholders. Among many projects, Ágata has leveraged electronic health records and predictive analytics to identify real-time health risks for pregnant women and newborns, saving thousands of lives. It has also integrated public financial management data across organizations, enabling them to visualize and avoid duplicating the services they provide to citizens, enhancing resource allocation. This case study demonstrates the value that a centralized analytics unit can bring to public administration.

(continues on next page)

TABLE 1.1 Summary of Case Studies *(continued)*

Country	Case study	Summary
Peru	3.9: Establishing a Decentralized Analytics Unit to Improve the Efficiency of Tax Collection	In Peru, tax compliance is a challenge for tax authorities. To address this challenge, the National Superintendency of Customs and Tax Administration created its own analytics unit. This unit has undertaken numerous analytical projects to strengthen tax and customs control and compliance, yielding millions of dollars in additional revenue and serving as a key element of the superintendency's strategy to improve the efficiency of tax administration. This case study demonstrates how decentralized analytics units can develop sophisticated predictive analytics, leading to significant improvements in tax revenue collection.
Multiple countries	3.10: Datathons as a Tool for Promoting Data Analytics	Many governments in Latin America and the Caribbean have established platforms or hosted events for sharing best practices, tools, and success stories related to analytics. At these "datathons," public servants and members of the community are given access to government data, learn about a relevant policy question, and collaborate to produce analytics that can be used to inform policy making. This case study demonstrates that governments benefit from engaging with data analysts inside and outside the public sector to gather ideas for analytical products and strengthen recruitment channels.
Brazil	3.11: The Power of Data Integration to Strengthen the Integrity of Public Procurement	In 2022, the World Bank piloted the Governance Risk Assessment System (GRAS) in Brazil. GRAS uses algorithms to identify patterns associated with public procurement fraud and corruption, targeting public suppliers, contracting agencies, and individual actors. A pillar of GRAS is its robust data integration framework, which aggregates, links, and analyzes large volumes of public procurement data, including detailed microdata on firms and individuals. During the pilot, GRAS identified about 800 firms that were awarded contracts despite legal sanctions and assisted federal police in uncovering networks of shell companies and money-laundering operations. This case study demonstrates how public sector corruption can be detected and reduced by integrating government data, applying descriptive and predictive analytics, and triangulating data.
Uruguay	3.12: Supporting the Implementation of Framework Agreements through Data Analytics	In 2019, the World Bank conducted a review of Uruguay's public procurement data that identified framework agreements as a strategy for improving the performance of the procurement system. During this review's implementation phase, analytics was useful for identifying items that could be purchased through framework agreements. This case study demonstrates the impact of descriptive and diagnostic analytics to identify suitable interventions and support their design during the implementation stage of a program.

Source: Original table for this publication.
Note: HealthMIS = health management information system; HRMIS = human resources management information system; TaxMIS = tax management information system.

TABLE 1.2 Key Findings and Policy Recommendations for Strengthening Government Analytics

a. *How can governments move toward a more strategic approach to government analytics to generate evidence for decision-making?*

Key findings	Policy recommendations
• When government analytics is fit for a particular purpose and tailored to specific policy needs, it can enhance decision-making and help achieve development outcomes. • Governments in Latin America and the Caribbean mainly use administrative data for descriptive analytics; diagnostic and predictive analytics remain underutilized. • Governments in the region mainly use analytical products for monitoring and accountability and, to a lesser extent, policy evaluation and design. • Governments in the region mainly use management information systems (MISs) for operational and transactional purposes, missing opportunities to use administrative data and advanced analytics to improve decision-making.	• **Strengthen the culture for evidence-based policy making and the demand for analytics within public administration.** Review how data are used in policy making. Define priorities for reform and the evidence needed to guide reforms. Build demand for analytics through workshops, conferences, and data-sharing programs. Foster interagency partnerships and implement data governance and management strategies. • **Define the strategic use of government data.** Review how administrative data analytics can inform decision-making in specific policy areas. Strategize regarding broader uses of data and consider how connected data can benefit multiple organizations. • **Streamline descriptive analytics and develop diagnostic and predictive analytics.** Create the conditions needed to use administrative data effectively for monitoring and accountability by defining a framework, establishing a reporting process, and creating a dissemination tool. Move toward diagnostic and predictive analytics to inform policy evaluation and design.

b. *How can governments build analytical capabilities for individuals and organizations?*

Key findings	Policy recommendations
• Although governments in Latin America and the Caribbean acknowledge the importance of analytical skills, they lack structured career tracks for data analysts and proficiency evaluations for public servants. • Funding for the development of analytical projects is limited in the region. • Creating dedicated analytics units and collaborating with academic or international organizations can be effective strategies for addressing capacity-building challenges and streamlining the use of analytics in decision-making.	• **Assess existing analytical capabilities.** Regularly assess public sector analytical capabilities to identify capacity-building needs. Develop plans to align workforce skills with those needed for strategic government analytics. • **Build analytical capabilities strategically.** Offer data analytics training tailored to the specific needs of decision-makers, analysts, and subject area experts. Develop a framework connecting skills development to practical applications. • **Establish a dedicated career track for data analysts to attract and retain talent.** • **Institutionalize government analytics.** Establish dedicated analytics units and secure a budget for supporting analytical capabilities and products. • **Develop external collaborations.** Forge external collaborations with academia, nonprofits, and multilateral organizations to address budget constraints and skills shortages and to facilitate the coproduction of analytical products through effective data-sharing frameworks.

(continues on next page)

TABLE 1.2 Key Findings and Policy Recommendations for Strengthening Government Analytics *(continued)*

c. *How can governments strengthen data infrastructure?*

Key findings	Policy recommendations
• Despite progress in digitalization, many MISs in Latin America and the Caribbean are not comprehensive enough or are inadequately updated, with considerable variation. • Measures for controlling data quality are not widely implemented in MISs in the region, and the manual, sporadic nature of data cleaning poses challenges for the accuracy, reliability, promptness, and replicability of analytics. • MIS interoperability is limited, and data sharing between government agencies is ad hoc, preventing governments from fully unlocking the potential of digitalized MISs for analytical projects.	• **Assess the quality, completeness, and timeliness of government data and define steps for improvement.** Regularly assess and update MISs and examine broader data ecosystems to prevent silos and strengthen MIS effectiveness. • **Establish regular, systematic, and automated data quality controls.** Embed data quality controls within MIS frameworks to ensure accuracy and reliability. Establish a dedicated team responsible for this. • **Establish a data inventory.** A data inventory should include available data types, storage locations, and field definitions. This simplifies project development and ensures proper data life cycle management. • **Connect government data.** Establish protocols for data sharing between government agencies to connect and integrate administrative data effectively. • **Plan for MIS maintenance and updates.** Create the conditions for MIS updates to continually leverage the newest technological advancements.

Source: Original table for this publication.

NOTES

1. Refer to table 1.1 and chapter 3 for detailed information on these and other analytical initiatives by governments in the region.
2. For instance, through the Global Evaluation Initiative, the World Bank is promoting global efforts to strengthen country systems for monitoring, evaluation, and use of evidence for decision-making. This includes the establishment of Regional Centers for Learning on Evaluation and Results in countries in Latin America and the Caribbean such as Brazil and Chile (GEI, n.d.-a, n.d.-b).
3. The report recognizes that other MISs are important for the effective functioning of public administration. However, it focuses on these six types of MISs because they are widely adopted in the region and represent the core functions of the executive branch of the state.
4. The World Bank has been a crucial partner for countries in Latin America and the Caribbean, supporting the design and implementation of initiatives to adopt or modernize MISs. These efforts have been particularly focused on public financial management information systems, because of the importance of modern systems for policy implementation and service delivery. By 2011, for example, 45 percent of the World Bank's projects in Latin America and the Caribbean included key investments in information and communication technology for financial management (Dener, Watkins, and Dorotinsky 2011; Pimenta and Pessoa 2016). These efforts reflect the World Bank's ongoing commitment to support governments in fostering data-driven decision-making through their MISs and in leveraging innovations in information and communication technology to improve policy implementation and service delivery.

REFERENCES

Best, Michael Carlos, Jonas Hjort, and David Szakonyi. 2023. "Individuals and Organizations as Sources of State Effectiveness." *American Economic Review* 113 (8): 2121–67. https://doi.org/10.1257/aer.20191598.

Bridges, Kate, and Michael Woolcock. 2023. "Measuring What Matters: Principles for a Balanced Data Suite That Prioritizes Problem Solving and Learning." In *The Government Analytics Handbook: Leveraging Data to Strengthen Public Administration*, edited by Daniel Rogger and Christian Schuster, chap. 4. Washington, DC: World Bank. https://doi.org/10.1596/978-1-4648-1957-5.

Dener, Cem, Joanna Alexandra Watkins, and William Leslie Dorotinsky. 2011. *Financial Management Information Systems: 25 Years of World Bank Experience on What Works and What Doesn't*. Washington, DC: World Bank. https://documents.worldbank.org/curated/en/485641468139212120/Financial-management-information-systems-25-years-of-World-Bank-experience-on-what-works-and-what-doesnt.

GEI (Global Evaluation Initiative). n.d.-a. "The CLEAR Network." GEI, World Bank. Accessed May 8, 2024. https://www.globalevaluationinitiative.org/clear-network.

GEI (Global Evaluation Initiative). n.d.-b. "Who We Are." GEI, World Bank. Accessed May 8, 2024. https://www.globalevaluationinitiative.org/who-we-are.

Hausmann, Ricardo, and Dani Rodrik. 2006. "Doomed to Choose: Industrial Policy as Predicament." Working paper, Center for International Development, Harvard University, Cambridge, MA. https://drodrik.scholar.harvard.edu/publications/doomed-choose-industrial-policy-predicament.

IMF (International Monetary Fund). 2021. *Regional Economic Outlook: Western Hemisphere; A Long and Winding Road to Recovery*. World Economic and Financial Surveys. Washington, DC: International Monetary Fund. https://www.imf.org/en/Publications/REO/WH/Issues/2021/10/21/Regional-Economic-Outlook-October-2021-Western-Hemisphere.

Izquierdo, Alejandro, Carola Pessino, and Guillermo Vuletin, eds. 2018. *Better Spending for Better Lives: How Latin America and the Caribbean Can Do More with Less*. Washington, DC: Inter-American Development Bank. https://dx.doi.org/10.18235/0001217-es.

Keefer, Philip, and Carlos Scartascini, eds. 2022. *Trust: The Key to Social Cohesion and Growth in Latin America and the Caribbean*. Washington, DC: Inter-American Development Bank. http://dx.doi.org/10.18235/0003911.

Maloney, William, Pablo Garriga, Marcela Meléndez, Raúl Morales, Charl Jooste, James Sampi, Jorge Thompson Araujo, and Ekaterina Vostroknutova. 2024. *Competition: The Missing Ingredient for Growth?* Latin America and the Caribbean Economic Review, April 2024. Washington, DC: World Bank. http://hdl.handle.net/10986/41230.

Mazzucato, Mariana, and Dani Rodrik. 2023. "Industrial Policy with Conditionalities: A Taxonomy and Sample Cases." Working Paper 2023/07, Institute for Innovation and Public Purpose, University College London. https://www.ucl.ac.uk/bartlett/public-purpose/wp2023-07.

Pimenta, Carlos, and Mario Pessoa, eds. 2016. *Public Financial Management in Latin America: The Key to Efficiency and Transparency*. Washington, DC: International Monetary Fund. https://doi.org/10.18235/0000083.

Rivas, Lisbeth, and Joe Crowley. 2018. "Using Administrative Data to Enhance Policymaking in Developing Countries: Tax Data and the National Accounts." IMF Working Paper 18/175, International Monetary Fund, Washington, DC. https://www.imf.org/en/Publications/WP/Issues/2018/08/02/Using-Administrative-Data-to-Enhance-Policymaking-in-Developing-Countries-Tax-Data-and-the-46054.

Rogger, Daniel, and Christian Schuster, eds. 2023. *The Government Analytics Handbook: Leveraging Data to Strengthen Public Administration*. Washington, DC: World Bank. https://doi.org/10.1596/978-1-4648-1957-5.

Statistics Canada. n.d. "Administrative Data." Accessed March 15, 2024. https://www.statcan.gc.ca/en/our-data/where/administrative-data.

UK Office for Statistics Regulation. n.d. "Administrative Data (Part 1)." Accessed March 15, 2024. https://osr.statisticsauthority.gov.uk/guidance/administrative-data-and-official-statistics/quality-assurance-of-administrative-data-case-examples/administrative-data-part-1/.

US Census Bureau. n.d. "Administrative Data." Accessed March 15, 2024. https://www.census.gov/topics/research/guidance/restricted-use-microdata/administrative-data.html.

World Bank. 2016. *World Development Report 2016: Digital Dividends*. Washington, DC: World Bank. https://doi.org/10.1596/978-1-4648-0671-1.

World Bank. 2021. *World Development Report 2021: Data for Better Lives*. Washington, DC: World Bank. https://www.worldbank.org/en/publication/wdr2021.

World Bank. 2022a. *GovTech Maturity Index, 2022 Update: Trends in Public Sector Digital Transformation*. Equitable Growth, Finance and Institutions Insight—Governance. Washington, DC: World Bank. https://hdl.handle.net/10986/38499.

World Bank. 2022b. *New Approaches to Closing the Fiscal Gap*. LAC Semiannual Update. Washington, DC: World Bank. https://hdl.handle.net/10986/38093.

World Bank. 2023. *Interoperability: Towards a Data-Driven Public Sector*. Equitable Growth, Finance and Institutions Insight—Governance. Washington, DC: World Bank. https://doi.org/10.1596/38520.

CHAPTER 2

A Conceptual Framework for Government Analytics

INTRODUCTION

Governments in Latin America and the Caribbean can deepen their use of government analytics to design and implement better public policy. To understand how to do so, practitioners first need to examine the broader context that shapes analytical initiatives. This chapter introduces a conceptual framework for assessing government analytics that describes how data and analytics can be used to improve government outcomes through evidence-based policy making and maps the enabling conditions for government analytics (figure 2.1).

Countries and government organizations in Latin America and the Caribbean vary considerably in the extent to which they analyze their administrative data, the types of analytics they undertake and the methodologies they employ, and the ways they apply analytics to address policy-making challenges. For this reason, the conceptual framework presented in this chapter is designed to be generalizable to different contexts. The conceptual framework informs this report's description of analytical initiatives in chapter 3, its empirical overview of analytics in the region in chapter 4, and the policy recommendations in chapter 5.

By assessing government analytics holistically, policy makers in the region can reflect on how they are using their administrative data and identify necessary steps to unlock its full potential. To make the conceptual framework more concrete and intuitive, this chapter points to real-world examples of analytical initiatives from the chapter 3 case studies. Online appendix C also includes a simulated example that puts readers in the position of an analyst looking for insights in human resources data. The case studies and the simulated example provide an accessible overview of government analytics and its enabling conditions, but readers who are interested in the more technical details of implementation are advised to consult *The Government Analytics*

A reproducibility package is available for this book in the Reproducible Research Repository at https://reproducibility.worldbank.org/index.php/catalog/209.

FIGURE 2.1 A Conceptual Framework for Government Analytics

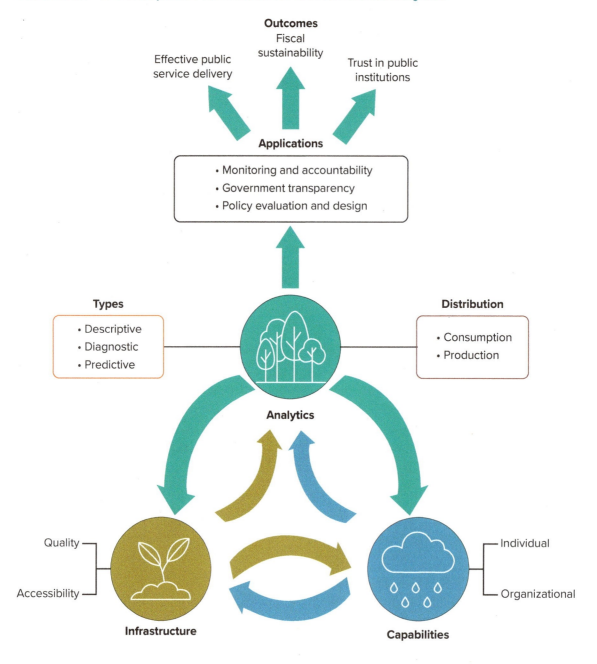

Source: Original figure for this publication.

Handbook (Rogger and Schuster 2023), which provides in-depth analytical guidance on specific government functions and information systems, such as human resources management, procurement, and public financial management.

In designing the conceptual framework, the chapter draws on evidence from research and policy reports, as well as survey instruments that measure governments' digital readiness (for instance, the Organisation for Economic Co-operation and Development's Survey on Digital Government, the United Nations' E-Government Survey, the World Bank's GovTech Maturity Index, and the Global Evaluation Initiative's Monitoring and Evaluation Systems Analysis tool). In this way, the chapter connects the conceptual and empirical analysis in this report to a wider policy agenda on the use of government technology in public administration and on government technology enablers and their analog complements, which serve as enabling factors for digital technologies (World Bank 2016, 2020, 2021, 2022b). The conceptual framework presented in this chapter makes government analytics concrete and actionable, offering governments a road map for applying its concepts in practice.

Government analytics should be developed and applied strategically, in response to real problems, demands, and needs. The first half of this chapter considers how analytics operates: what types of analytics governments can undertake, how analytical insights can be used to guide policy and decision-making, and how analytics is produced and consumed within public administration. The second half lays out the enabling conditions for producing and using analytics: the analytical capabilities and data infrastructure that make analytics of administrative data possible and ensure it can be used to address policy-making challenges across public administration. Creating these conditions is essential to making analytics part of the decision-making culture in public administration and deepening evidence-based policy making.

HOW DOES GOVERNMENT ANALYTICS IMPROVE GOVERNMENT FUNCTIONING?

To understand how governments use data to improve their functioning, this chapter first identifies the *types* of analytics that governments conduct, how governments *apply* analytics in their work, and how analytics is *distributed* among stakeholders within public administration and beyond.

What Types of Analytics Do Governments Conduct?

Government analytics can give rise to many types of initiatives. Analytics can help public servants target a reminder program to reduce missed medical appointments (case study 3.1) or help procurement 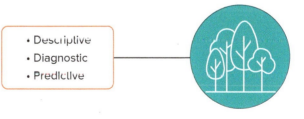 officers do their work more effectively (case study 3.7). It might even ground the creation of a "smart city" (case study 3.8). These initiatives range widely in their complexity and goals, but data experts typically categorize data analytics into three types: *descriptive*, *diagnostic*, and *predictive* (refer, for instance, to Cote 2021).[1]

Descriptive Analytics

Descriptive analytics is a foundational type of analytics. In the context of government analytics, it refers to the use of data to describe the public sector and illustrate broader trends. It might also summarize and present data to make analytical insights accessible to decision-makers. In general, descriptive analytics answers questions like the following:

- What happened? (In procurement, for instance: What did the government purchase?)
- When and how often did it happen? (For instance: How are government purchases distributed throughout the year?)
- Where did it happen? (For instance: How are purchases distributed across regions?)
- What are the principal characteristics or features of the data? (For instance: What is the average price paid for government purchases by product type?)

Descriptive analytics of administrative data involves the application of statistical techniques, including disaggregated percentages and ratios, simple correlations illustrating the relationship between variables, and cross-tabulations enabling the comparison of variables. Data visualization tools can also be used to communicate the results of the analysis to policy makers and the public through dashboards, graphs, and maps.

Descriptive analytics is an essential first step that makes analytical insights and evidence available to policy makers, laying the foundation for evidence-based policy making. In Chile, for example, the Ministry of Health designed a program that reduced missed medical appointments and increased primary care use by about 10 percent among its target population by using descriptive analytics to better understand the characteristics and needs of the patients who were missing appointments the most (case study 3.1).

Diagnostic Analytics

Diagnostic analytics builds on descriptive analytics by trying to understand not just *what* is happening but *why* it is happening. Whereas descriptive analytics identifies and illuminates trends in the public sector, diagnostic analytics determines the causes behind these trends using statistical models. In general, diagnostic analytics answers questions like the following:

- Why did this happen? (For instance: Why is competition low in public procurement?)
- What factors influenced this result? (For instance: What influences competition in public procurement?)

Diagnostic analytics builds on descriptive analytics by enabling public officials to identify causal mechanisms that explain the trends they observe in data. For example, in Colombia, the Data Scientists Unit of the National Planning Department analyzed data from human resources management information systems (HRMISs) using a combination of descriptive and diagnostic analytics to understand the causes of wage differentials in the public sector and discovered a gender pay gap of about 6 percent among temporary workers. This enabled the department to assess de facto compliance with Colombia's gender antidiscrimination law and inform the relevant national authority so it could act on the findings (case study 3.2).

Predictive Analytics

Predictive analytics is the most complex type of analytics. It uses historical data and statistical modeling techniques, informed by an understanding of causal mechanisms, to make predictions about what will happen in the future and how individuals or organizations are likely to respond to actions and interventions. These predictions enable governments to be proactive and apply a deeper understanding of future consequences to present-day decisions. In general, predictive analytics answers questions like the following:

- What is likely to happen in the future? (For instance: How much is the government likely to spend in each sector in the future?)

- What is the probability that a specific event will occur? (For instance: How likely is it that a contract will be renegotiated?)

Predictive analytics builds on descriptive and diagnostic analytics because it combines a data-driven picture of the current state of the public sector (provided by descriptive analytics) with a deep understanding of the causal mechanisms driving trends (provided by diagnostic analytics) to make informed predictions.

For example, the federal government of Brazil and the World Bank used predictive analytics to project the government wage bill under different policy scenarios. These projections considered headcount growth, salary progression, and other factors to simulate wage bill growth while modeling the effects of reducing wage growth, hiring freezes, and other policies (figure 2.2). These projections informed a redesign of the federal government's wage policy, providing a clear justification for wage adjustments to avert a fiscal crisis (Tavares, Ortega Nieto, and Woodhouse 2023).

FIGURE 2.2 Cumulative Fiscal Savings in Three Wage Bill Policy Scenarios, Brazil, 2019–30

Source: Tavares, Ortega Nieto, and Woodhouse 2023, based on Brazilian government data from 2019.

For examples of different types of analytics using administrative data, refer to chapters 10–12, 14, and 15 of *The Government Analytics Handbook.*

Classifying different analytical initiatives as descriptive, diagnostic, or predictive helps practitioners better understand how each type of analytics complements the others. For example, results from descriptive analytics can highlight the need for more in-depth analysis through diagnostic or predictive analytics. Likewise, a well-designed dashboard that helps users visualize and interpret trends in the data (descriptive analytics) could be enhanced with features that help evaluate the possible outcomes of different scenarios (predictive analytics). Governments require more sophisticated capabilities and infrastructure to undertake more advanced analytics. Nevertheless, descriptive analytics may be sufficient for questions that require straightforward measurement to answer, and it also provides the high-quality foundation required for more complex analytical tasks. For instance, descriptive analytics enabled the youth anticorruption organization reAcción Paraguay to track government spending on schools, increasing government accountability to citizens (case study 3.3).

Governments should recognize the types of analytics they can already produce as well as identify next steps to build their capacity and infrastructure for more complex analytics, without losing sight of the kinds of questions that will be useful to policy makers. Each type of analytics serves the overarching goal of transforming raw data into actionable information, each type of analytics depends on the others, and each type of analytics can be applied to strengthen government functioning.

How Do Governments Apply Analytics?

After the types of analytics a government is undertaking have been assessed, the focus can turn to *how* it applies analytics to enhance policy design and implementation. The report's conceptual framework identifies three general applications of government analytics: to enable *monitoring and accountability*, to increase *government transparency*, and to aid in *policy evaluation and design*.

- Monitoring and accountability
- Government transparency
- Policy evaluation and design

Monitoring and Accountability

The first application of government analytics considered here is to enable *monitoring and accountability*. Analytics can be used to report on the status quo within public administration, monitor trends, track progress toward goals, and hold public officials accountable. For example, analytics can be used to design tools aimed at identifying fraud and corruption. In procurement, this could mean implementing a system that flags irregularities in bidding contracts (case study 3.11).[2] As another example, in Uruguay, the National Civil Service Office is developing an online human resources management platform that will enable strategic workforce planning by making information on the composition of the public sector workforce, the skills and competencies within it, and future human capital needs more accessible to decision-makers (case study 3.4).

To successfully use analytics for monitoring and accountability, governments must be mindful of communication. Using analytics for monitoring can lead to pervasive distrust among public servants, particularly if governments do not clearly communicate how data will be used. Careless communication can foster the perception that analytics is a tool for control rather than a means to foster accountability and efficiency, hindering the successful introduction of analytical innovations in the public sector.

For examples of how analytics can be used for monitoring and accountability to reduce corruption, refer to chapter 8 of *The Government Analytics Handbook*.

Government Transparency

The second application of government analytics this section considers is to increase *government transparency*. When citizens have access to actionable information about how government operates—for instance, through a dashboard or portal that tracks service delivery or public investment in different regions of a country—they are empowered to hold the government accountable, identify policy issues, communicate their priorities, and advocate for change.

The organization reAcción Paraguay demonstrates how citizen mobilization, empowered by publicly available data from the country's e-Procurement system, brought to light mismanagement of public funds, helped the government improve the allocation of public resources, and generated momentum to make the implementation and management of public programs more transparent and accountable to the public (case study 3.3). Using analytics to increase government transparency aligns closely with policy goals regarding open government, open data, and citizen engagement (World Bank 2022a).

Policy Evaluation and Design

The final application of government analytics considered here is to guide *policy evaluation and design*. Using analytics for policy evaluation is a growing agenda with wide-ranging applications across different areas of government (refer, for example, to Legovini and Jones 2021). External actors can also contribute to these applications. Granting research institutions and universities access to administrative data not only increases transparency but can also fuel a research agenda to help policy makers investigate the effects of existing policies, evaluate their cost-effectiveness, and gain a clearer understanding of the mechanisms underlying their effects.

Administrative data analytics can be a low-cost option for policy evaluation, potentially overcoming the lack of baseline data for long-running programs (Barca et al. 2023). For example, researchers working with the tax authority in Ecuador analyzed tax data to evaluate a policy intervention in which firms were notified about revenue discrepancies in their tax reports, demonstrating under what conditions the policy was effective in increasing corporate tax collection (case study 3.5).

Government analytics can also guide the development and design of new policies. Analytics can be integrated into the design of programs to help governments leverage existing resources efficiently, ensuring that programs are cost-effective before they are implemented more widely. In Guatemala, the Ministry of Education piloted a program incorporating analytics to improve education service delivery. By using predictive analytics to produce lists of students at risk of dropping out of school, the ministry enabled school staff to identify and support these students. An impact evaluation of the program measured its effectiveness in a few schools within the country before it was scaled up nationwide (case study 3.6).

How Is Government Analytics Distributed?

Even if government analytics is highly advanced and its goals are clearly defined, it will not contribute to improving government functioning unless it is actively used by policy makers and other stakeholders. Assessing

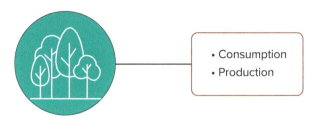

- Consumption
- Production

the impact of analytics requires understanding the extent of its *consumption* and *production*, including identifying current and potential users of analytical products. To have an impact, analytics must be produced in response to a specific policy need identified by its consumers.

Consumption

The first factor considered here is who *consumes* analytical products in the public sector and why. Understanding analytics consumption makes it possible to identify whether the knowledge being generated is relevant to the people who use it—and thus whether it is useful for shaping critical decisions. For instance, analytics on primary school students' learning trajectories might help an early childhood development agency refine its pedagogical decisions, but it might not be relevant (especially in the short run) to a higher education agency.

At the same time, different government agents might use the same analytical products for different purposes. For example, politicians might use analytics to design more effective laws and policies, while public sector managers might use it to assess the performance of their units. Understanding who uses an analytical product and adapting the product in response to their feedback is crucial to ensure that analytics remains relevant to the needs of policy makers. Likewise, taking a broad view of the *potential* consumers of analytical products can help governments understand the need for evidence among different decision-makers across public administration, enabling them to identify opportunities for analytical solutions and better target and implement those solutions. Analytics has more impact when policy makers ask for the evidence they need and use it to shape policies and inform critical decisions, which requires a deeper culture of evidence-based decision-making.

By understanding and responding to existing operational needs, analytics producers may even discover new uses for existing analytics. For example, the tax team at the Secretariat of Finance of Rio Grande do Sul state in Brazil developed an algorithm that uses tax data from electronic business-to-business invoices to estimate market reference prices. This algorithm initially served a descriptive function within the tax unit. But its value increased dramatically when it was shared with procurement teams, who were able to use the market reference price information to enhance their negotiation strategies, leading to a significant reduction—13.2 percent—in the price of procured goods (case study 3.7). When analytical products are shared and adapted by producers to meet the needs of consumers, new types and applications of analytics can be uncovered.

 For an outline of how policy makers can consume and disseminate analytical products, refer to chapters 25 and 26 of *The Government Analytics Handbook*.

Production

The second element examined here is how often agencies *produce* analytics. Even high quality, much-needed analytics, if only produced intermittently or when it is already too late to inform policy decisions, will not be useful to decision-makers. For example, imagine an agency that produces stellar predictive analytics about the evolution of the government's wage bill—but does so only when it is already too late to inform budget discussions.

Three different kinds of analytics production can be identified. Analytics can be produced *ad hoc*, in the form of single exercises in response to one-off requests. It can also be produced on a more regular basis in a *bureaucratic* fashion, to comply with existing laws and regulations. Finally, analytics can be produced *strategically*, in the form of continuous analytical products that respond to an overall strategic plan to meet organizational needs and respond to real-time demands.

A strategic approach to producing analytics is essential to getting useful information into the hands of decision-makers when they need it most. If agencies produce analytics on a regular schedule, it is easier to disseminate information to those who need it and integrate evidence into existing decision-making processes. Strategically producing analytics also helps decision-makers think proactively about the evidence they need to guide policies and reforms, and it can even help them identify problems or opportunities they would not otherwise notice, making it easier to build toward more complex analytics. For example, continually monitoring health indicators enabled the Ministry of Health of Chile to discover that the patients who need regular medical checkups most—those with chronic conditions—were missing primary care appointments more frequently, a problem they had not previously identified. This insight enabled the ministry to take appropriate action to address the issue (case study 3.1).

How Do the Types, Applications, and Distribution of Analytics Interact?

What analytics looks like needs to be broken down in this level of detail because it is possible to pursue each of the applications of government analytics—enabling monitoring and accountability, increasing government transparency, and aiding policy evaluation and design—using descriptive, diagnostic, and predictive types of analytics. It is also possible to pursue them at different scales of production and consumption: an analytical project might be targeted at a specific government agency or aim to reach a government-wide audience, including public sector managers and politicians. For example, consider a dashboard tracking data regarding service delivery. This is a descriptive analytics application, but it might be applied differently by different stakeholders. A government agency might use the dashboard to monitor its own efficiency, whereas a watchdog organization might use it to evaluate government transparency, and policy makers might consult it when making budget decisions. For this reason, practitioners need to consider the types, applications, and distribution of government analytics to describe it holistically.

These independent dimensions of analytics also interact. Governments should tailor the types of analytics they produce to the operational needs of its current and potential users. Likewise, they should consider how different types and applications of analytics can build on one another, especially when analytical products are regularly produced, shared, and improved. However, understanding how different types of analytics are produced and consumed within public administration and applied to address different policy-making challenges illustrates only a piece of the overall government analytics ecosystem. Analytics also interacts with its enabling conditions: the underlying factors that make analytical projects possible and help them succeed in improving government functioning. The following section discusses two essential enabling conditions for government analytics: analytical capabilities and data infrastructure.

WHAT ENABLING CONDITIONS SUPPORT GOVERNMENT ANALYTICS?

An understanding of what analytics looks like in public administration—including what types of analytics are produced and how they are applied—provides a starting point for a deeper exploration of the enabling conditions for analytics. What factors make government analytics possible and enable it to have an impact with respect to improving decision-making and public policy? By defining and identifying these factors, governments can map opportunities to build capacity in the directions outlined in the previous section—toward more diverse types of analytics, more intensive and strategic production of analytics, and more extensive application of analytics by decision-makers—all while ensuring that analytics remains problem driven and relevant to policy makers' needs.

The discussion here first examines the analytical *capabilities* governments need, focusing on strategies and actions at both the organizational and individual levels to promote and sustain the use of analytics. Second, it considers the data *infrastructure* that ensures data are high in quality and readily accessible to analytics teams and decision-makers (figure 2.3).

FIGURE 2.3 Enabling Conditions for Government Analytics

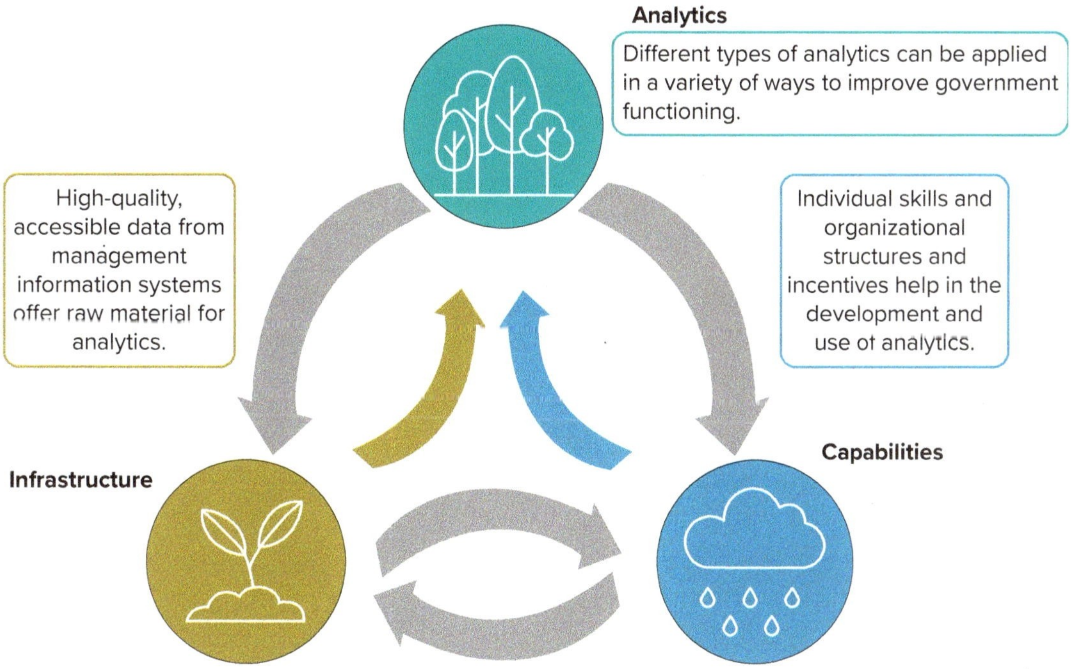

Analytics
Different types of analytics can be applied in a variety of ways to improve government functioning.

High-quality, accessible data from management information systems offer raw material for analytics.

Individual skills and organizational structures and incentives help in the development and use of analytics.

Infrastructure

Capabilities

Source: Original figure for this publication.

What Analytical Capabilities Does the Government Possess?

The underlying capabilities required for data analytics and evidence-based policy making include not just individual skills but also the institutional structures and incentives that support the development and use of analytical insights. Analytical capabilities can thus be categorized as either *organizational* or *individual*.

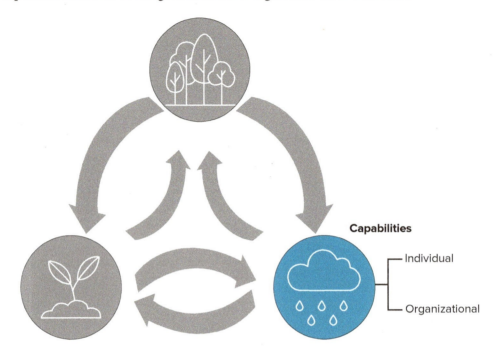

Organizational Capabilities

Structures, incentives, and strategies at the organizational level play a critical role in promoting and sustaining the use of analytics as a key decision-making tool. Dedicated analytics units, incentives to support analytical projects, and strategies for collaborating with external actors create conditions in which decision-makers have easy access to high-quality analytics when they need it. Governments that proactively invest in their analytical capabilities are more likely to use data effectively overall (Pew Charitable Trusts 2018).

Dedicated analytics units are instrumental in promoting the production of analytics and ensuring that analytics insights align closely with operational needs, as discussed in the previous section. These units not only centralize expertise but also foster a more cohesive and agile approach to using analytical products to tackle policy challenges. Without them, analytics efforts tend to be ad hoc, making it challenging to strategically and consistently produce analytics that meet organizational demands and the needs of decision-makers.

Analytics units can be organized in a centralized manner, with a single, dedicated analytics unit in the government responsible for producing analytics across diverse government functions and information systems in response to the needs and demands of different agencies. For example, the Ágata data analytics unit in Bogotá, Colombia, is responsible for generating insights across different policy areas, including health and public finance, to support Bogotá's transformation into a "smart city" (case study 3.8).

Alternatively, a government might operate under a decentralized model in which individual agencies invest in developing their own analytical teams to meet their own needs. For example, in Peru, the National Superintendency of Customs and Tax Administration has its own analytics unit. This unit has undertaken numerous analytical projects to improve tax and customs control and compliance, serving as a key element of the superintendency's strategy for improving the efficiency of tax administration (case study 3.9). While centralized analytics units can achieve economies of scale by enabling larger and more diverse teams, decentralized units may offer sector-specific knowledge relevant to better targeting of analytical products. However they are organized, analytics units allow governments to institutionalize analytical innovation and experimentation.

Governments can further encourage the use of data analytics through incentives, including recognition programs, and by allocating funding to analytics. Internal funding opportunities for analytical projects can motivate agencies and public servants to explore innovative applications of data and analytics. Governments can also establish platforms or host events for sharing best practices, tools, and success stories, underscoring the significance of using analytics in enhancing outcomes. For example, governments in Ecuador and other countries in Latin America and the Caribbean are hosting special events for data analytics enthusiasts. At these "datathons," public servants and members of the public are given access to administrative data, which they use to identify relevant policy questions and produce analytics that can be used to inform policy making and improve government functioning (case study 3.10).

Strategies for collaborating with external actors also play a pivotal role in fostering a supportive environment for analytics. These strategies may include partnerships with researchers, academic institutions, nonprofits, or multilateral organizations. Among other initiatives, governments can collaborate with such organizations to obtain technical support for specific analytical projects, enhance data management practices, engage in analytical capacity-building activities, and integrate new analytical methods and products into their operations.

For guidance on how organizational reforms can enable government analytics, refer to chapter 3 of *The Government Analytics Handbook*.

Individual Capabilities

To build individual capabilities for analytics, governments must consider how to assess and strengthen the analytical skills of public servants, as well as how to recruit and retain data analysts. A mixture of subject area and analytical expertise is often necessary to ensure that analytical products will be relevant to decision-makers in a particular policy area (Bhupatiraju et al. 2023). Fostering this combination of expertise is a management challenge, however, especially in light of increasing job specialization.

In some contexts, it may be possible to train subject area experts, such as tax specialists, to conduct analytics on data in their field. Another approach is to create working groups (or units) that bring together subject area experts and data analysts to collaborate on analytical products. In this case, subject area experts must be able to articulate the evidence they need, understand analytical insights, and apply analytics to guide their decision-making. Which of these two approaches is better depends on an administration's existing skills and organizational capabilities, especially whether it has dedicated analytics units.

To choose an approach, governments also need to assess the analytical skills of public servants more broadly. Assessment tools like exams, focus groups, and surveys can help determine which analytical skills public servants have or need to develop. Governments must invest in ongoing training to support these skills, because the process of building analytical capacity requires time, while personnel turnover poses a challenge to the sustainability of increased capabilities.

Governments should also evaluate their recruitment practices and career advancement opportunities for data analysts, which determine whether they are adequately staffed with public servants capable of using data for analytics. Governments can signal their commitment to analytics and provide incentives for skilled data analysts to join and remain in the public sector by establishing a dedicated career track for data analysts. Having a dedicated career track also places public administration in a stronger position to capitalize on the potential of administrative data and emerging technologies. Research suggests, for example, that government organizations that consider technical or data skills key attributes when hiring public servants are better able to integrate and use new technologies to improve their operational effectiveness (Lember, Kattel, and Tõnurist 2018).

In addition to building analytical skills and recruiting and retaining data analysts, governments should consider initiatives to build decision-makers' capacity to use analytical products. Improving decision-makers' knowledge and ability to comprehend data analytics results—and identify their limitations—is crucial for effectively integrating analytical findings into decision-making processes (refer, for example, to Hjort et al. 2021; Mehmood, Naseer, and Chen 2024).

What Is the State of the Government's Data Infrastructure?

Governments' organizational and individual capabilities to undertake, manage, and apply data analytics and its insights are important, but analytics will not lead to better outcomes unless the data on which it is built are high in *quality* and *accessible* (US Commission on Evidence-Based Policymaking 2017).[3] Effective data management includes the creation and establishment of protocols to guarantee data quality, accessibility, interoperability, and relevance, along with government agencies to oversee these protocols. It is also crucial to ensure that data are used ethically and transparently. Laws and regulations ensuring citizens control their own data can foster transparency and increase the demand for government analytics among public servants and citizens (Attard et al. 2015; World Bank 2021).

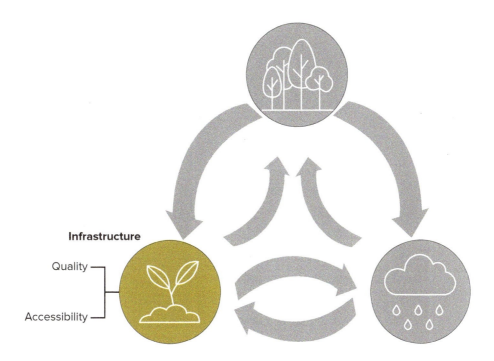

Data Quality

High-quality data are accurate (they represent reality as closely as possible), complete (they are not missing any critical information), consistent (they adhere to the same standards and formats across records and over time), and reliable (repeated analyses of the same data points produce similar results).

Establishing robust, systematic data quality controls is the first step toward harnessing administrative data for analytics. Management information systems typically function as central repositories for transactional data: they collect and process the daily operations of government organizations. For example, an e-Procurement system registers contracts for government purchases, and a public financial management information system (PFMIS) collects data about budget allocations to programs. Since administrative data are not usually collected and compiled with analytical purposes in mind, guaranteeing the quality of these data and their readiness for analytics is particularly important to ensure high-quality analytical products.

The processes for preparing administrative data for analytics demand investments in technical infrastructure, including software and hardware, as well as skilled personnel. The critical task of "cleaning" data, for instance, includes identifying and correcting duplicates, corrupt observations, inaccuracies, and inconsistencies. It is also important to ensure that data adhere to standardized formats to facilitate harmonization and interoperability across various data sets and information systems.[4]

Finally, anonymization or pseudonymization techniques are necessary to meet data protection and privacy standards.[5]

Linking or integrating data from different sources through common data identifiers is another way to increase data relevance, make data more usable, and increase the impact of analytical products. For example, the World Bank, in collaboration with subnational governments in Brazil, developed an innovative, data-driven tool to improve the detection of fraud, corruption, and collusion in public procurement. This tool, known as the Governance Risk Assessment System, depends on the integration of diverse data sources, including e-Procurement systems and HRMISs, with corporate and shareholder information. The risk assessment system proved instrumental in investigating procurement irregularities in Brazil (case study 3.11).

For principles and guidance on strengthening data infrastructure, especially that for data from human resources management information systems and public financial management information systems, refer to chapters 9 and 11 of *The Government Analytics Handbook*.

Data Accessibility

High-quality data must be accessible and promptly available to have an impact on government functioning. Data accessibility means that public servants can regularly access data owned by their organizations, that data and analytical products are readily shared within government, and that data are made available to the public, all while adhering to protocols for confidentiality and ethics.[6]

When data are accessible and readily available, they enable analysts, policy makers, and researchers to harness a wealth of information that can drive informed decisions. For example, the Secretariat of Finance of Rio Grande do Sul state in Brazil was able to design an algorithm to guide procurement based on administrative data that had originally been collected for taxation. The integration of data across different information systems created the conditions for collaboration across units, resulting in an innovative analytical product that decreased procurement prices by 13.2 percent (case study 3.7).

Administrative data are valuable not only for internal analytics but also for external sharing to promote transparency, transforming data into a public asset. In this context, the open data movement has been pivotal in facilitating public access to data for transparency and civic engagement. Paraguay, for instance, was the first country in the world to create a portal adhering to the Open Government Partnership's Open Contracting Data Standard for publication and access to data on government contracts and public tenders (World Bank 2018). Data from this portal empowered the organization reAcción Paraguay to mobilize citizens and help the government improve the allocation of public resources (case study 3.3). When data are accessible to the public, transparency, accountability, and public trust are all enhanced because government actions and policies can be examined and validated.

These potential applications of administrative data are hampered by accessibility challenges. Inconsistent procedures and legal frameworks for data access and sharing (both within government and with outside parties), coupled with insufficient information about available data sets and their elements, hinder collaboration and innovation. When valuable data remain siloed within government agencies, it is difficult to cross-reference information and capture the full picture of a particular policy issue.

One way to tackle these challenges is to create a standardized process for analysts and policy makers to use to access administrative data. This entails, among other things, improving how data are managed and documented. For instance, establishing a comprehensive data inventory that outlines the available data sets and elements within information systems ensures that analysts and policy makers understand what information exists. In addition, detailed, searchable metadata documents can help users understand data characteristics, such as time frames, measurement units, and coverage. This enables users to assess the utility of the data for addressing policy questions before accessing them, so users can determine whether gaining access is worthwhile. Finally, a formal, well-documented, and easy-to-follow protocol should be put in place to regulate data access and security. By emphasizing data accessibility and simplifying protocols for their use, governments can markedly improve their analytical products.

How Do Analytical Capabilities and Data Infrastructure Interact?

The enabling conditions for government analytics—the individual and organizational capabilities and underlying data infrastructure—are the essential ingredients for every analytical project. But they are also the factors that make public administration a fruitful environment for evidence-based policy making in general: the kind of place where public servants are aware of the data that governments produce and work with, empowered to identify and undertake new analytical projects, and skilled at using analytical insights to make decisions, implement policies, and deliver goods and services with greater effectiveness and efficiency. Investment in analytical capabilities and data infrastructure can ensure public administration offers this kind of environment.

These enabling conditions also strengthen one another. The quality and accessibility of data infrastructure are strengthened by the skills of personnel who prepare data for analytics and the organizations that oversee quality and accessibility protocols. Likewise, stronger data infrastructure that links or integrates data from different sources makes higher-quality data accessible to organizations and individuals, enabling them to further develop their skills and undertake more complex analytics.

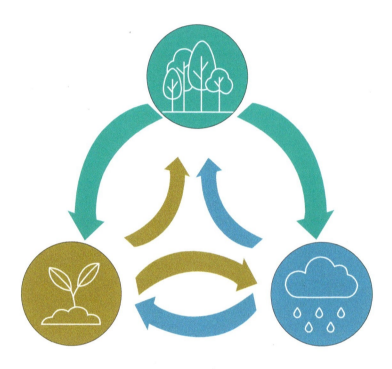

However, governments do not need to wait for the perfect set of enabling conditions to start undertaking analytics with administrative data. In fact, as this chapter has shown, good analytical projects not only produce decision-making insights but also help strengthen the enabling conditions for analytics within public administration. Analytical projects can help reveal weaknesses in the infrastructure for the data underlying the analysis, enabling improvements to be made. At the same time, undertaking an analytical project can help organizations identify the analytical skills their personnel need to develop, as well as the organizational structures and incentives that would make future projects more effective. When data are regularly produced by dedicated teams and consumed by decision-makers who offer feedback, next steps to further strengthen the enabling conditions for analytics are easier to identify. The next chapter looks at how some analytical initiatives in Latin America and the Caribbean have both drawn on and strengthened data infrastructure and analytical capabilities within public administration, all while improving government functioning across various policy areas.

NOTES

1. Data experts commonly acknowledge a fourth type, referred to as *prescriptive* analytics. However, given the overlap in definition with the other three types, this report does not treat it as a separate category.
2. Beyond its use for monitoring and accountability in specific sectors or policy areas, government analytics can also be applied to monitoring systems (commonly known as "monitoring and evaluation") at the national level. Centralized monitoring systems track progress toward the achievement of medium- or long-term objectives established in national strategies. Government data represent a rich source of information for national monitoring systems, especially for measuring how the functioning of public administration contributes to the achievement of broader development objectives.
3. Given the availability of high-quality consulting materials on data infrastructure, this section of the conceptual framework offers only a broad view of this important enabling condition. Notes provide references to companion pieces that provide the necessary details for readers seeking a more comprehensive exploration of the topics discussed.
4. For insights on systems interoperability and data harmonization, refer to *Interoperability: Towards a Data-Driven Public Sector* (World Bank 2023).
5. It is important to note that even if administrative data are of high quality, they may not have an architecture that allows policy makers or researchers to effectively use them. This issue is particularly significant with regard to personally identifiable information, as data files often need to be encrypted both in transit and at rest to protect privacy, imposing additional constraints on how the data are managed and used. Sharing encrypted data across agencies can be problematic if there are no standardized encryption protocols or agreements on data access and use. Data governance authorities should ensure that there are clear rules and procedures that facilitate analytics while protecting privacy. For insights on data governance, refer to chapters 6 and 8 of the *World Development Report 2021: Data for Better Lives* (World Bank 2021).
6. For insights on institutions, laws, and regulations to improve data accessibility, refer to the *GovTech Maturity Index, 2022 Update: Trends in Public Sector Digital Transformation* (World Bank 2022a).

REFERENCES

Attard, Judie, Fabrizio Orlandi, Simon Scerri, and Sören Auer. 2015. "A Systematic Review of Open Government Data Initiatives." *Government Information Quarterly* 32 (4): 399–418. https://doi.org/10.1016/j.giq.2015.07.006.

Barca, Valentina, Madhumitha Hebbar, Charles Knox-Vydamov, and Ida Brzezinska. 2023. "We Have the Data, Let's Use It Better: Pushing the Boundaries of Social Protection Administrative Data Analysis and Use." Deutsche Gesellschaft für Internationale Zusammenarbeit (GIZ) GmbH, Bonn, Germany. https://socialprotection.org/sites/default/files/publications_files/GIZ-%20Use%20Admin%20Data%20Social%20Protection.pdf.

Bhupatiraju, Sandeep, Daniel Chen, Slava Jankin, Galileu Kim, Maximilian Kupi, and Manuel Ramos Maqueda. 2023. "Government Analytics Using Machine Learning." In *The Government Analytics Handbook: Leveraging Data to Strengthen Public Administration*, edited by Daniel Rogger and Christian Schuster, chap. 16. Washington, DC: World Bank. https://doi.org/10.1596/978-1-4648-1957-5.

Cote, Catherine. 2021. "4 Types of Data Analytics to Improve Decision-Making." *Business Insights* (blog), October 19, 2021. https://online.hbs.edu/blog/post/types-of-data-analysis.

Hjort, Jonas, Diana Moreira, Gautam Rao, and Juan Francisco Santini. 2021. "How Research Affects Policy: Experimental Evidence from 2,150 Brazilian Municipalities." *American Economic Review* 111 (5): 1442–80. https://doi.org/10.1257/aer.20190830.

Legovini, Arianna, and Maria Ruth Jones. 2021. "Administrative Data in Research at the World Bank: The Case of Development Impact Evaluation (DIME)." In *Handbook on Using Administrative Data for Research and Evidence-Based Policy*, edited by Shawn Cole, Iqbal Dhaliwal, Anja Sautmann, and Lars Vilhuber, chap. 14. Cambridge, MA: Abdul Latif Jameel Poverty Action Lab. https://admindatahandbook.mit.edu/book/v1.0-rc6/dime.html.

Lember, Veiko, Rainer Kattel, and Piret Tõnurist. 2018. "Technological Capacity in the Public Sector: The Case of Estonia." *International Review of Administrative Sciences* 84 (2): 214–30. https://doi.org/10.1177/0020852317735164.

Mehmood, Sultan, Shaheen Naseer, and Daniel L. Chen. 2024. "Training Policymakers in Econometrics." Unpublished manuscript, last modified January 2024. https://users.nber.org/~dlchen/papers/Training_Policy_Makers_in_Econometrics.pdf.

Pew Charitable Trusts. 2018. *How States Use Data to Inform Decisions: A National Review of the Use of Administrative Data to Improve State Decision-Making*. Philadelphia: Pew Charitable Trusts. https://www.pewtrusts.org/en/research-and-analysis/reports/2018/02/how-states-use-data-to-inform-decisions.

Rogger, Daniel, and Christian Schuster, eds. 2023. *The Government Analytics Handbook: Leveraging Data to Strengthen Public Administration*. Washington, DC: World Bank. https://doi.org/10.1596/978-1-4648-1957-5.

Tavares, Rafael Alves de Albuquerque, Daniel Ortega Nieto, and Eleanor Florence Woodhouse. 2023. "Government Analytics Using Human Resources and Payroll Data." In *The Government Analytics Handbook: Leveraging Data to Strengthen Public Administration*, edited by Daniel Rogger and Christian Schuster, chap. 10. Washington, DC: World Bank. https://doi.org/10.1596/978-1-4648-1957-5_ch10.

US Commission on Evidence-Based Policymaking. 2017. *The Promise of Evidence-Based Policymaking: Report of the Commission on Evidence-Based Policymaking*. Report to the President of the United States, Speaker of the House, and President of the Senate. https://www2.census.gov.mcas.ms/adrm/fesac/2017-12-15/Abraham-CEP-final-report.pdf.

World Bank. 2016. *World Development Report 2016: Digital Dividends*. Washington, DC: World Bank. https://doi.org/10.1596/978-1-4648-0671-1.

World Bank. 2018. "Paraguay: Systematic Country Diagnostic." World Bank, Washington, DC. https://documents1.worldbank.org/curated/en/827731530819395899/pdf/Paraguay-SCD-06292018.pdf.

World Bank. 2020. *Digital Government Readiness Assessment (DGRA) Toolkit V.31: Guidelines for Task Teams*. Version 3.0 (April 2020). Washington, DC: World Bank.

World Bank. 2021. *World Development Report 2021: Data for Better Lives*. Washington, DC: World Bank. https://www.worldbank.org/en/publication/wdr2021.

World Bank. 2022a. *GovTech Maturity Index, 2022 Update: Trends in Public Sector Digital Transformation*. Equitable Growth, Finance and Institutions Insight—Governance. Washington, DC: World Bank. https://hdl.handle.net/10986/38499.

World Bank. 2022b. *New Approaches to Closing the Fiscal Gap*. LAC Semiannual Update. Washington, DC: World Bank. https://hdl.handle.net/10986/38093.

World Bank. 2023. *Interoperability: Towards a Data-Driven Public Sector*. Equitable Growth, Finance and Institutions Insight—Governance. Washington, DC: World Bank. https://doi.org/10.1596/38520.

CHAPTER 3

Case Studies of Government Analytics in Latin America and the Caribbean

INTRODUCTION

The conceptual framework presented in the previous chapter offers a high-level view of the different elements that make up the government analytics ecosystem, which practitioners can use to understand how analytical initiatives succeed in enhancing policy design and implementation. This chapter addresses this question by offering detailed descriptions of 12 case studies of analytical initiatives in Latin America and the Caribbean, covering various countries and policy areas. Each case study provides an example of how government and citizen organizations have used administrative data to generate evidence for decision-making and the significant impact of this evidence on how policy challenges are addressed. The case studies also consider how enabling conditions (data infrastructure and analytical capabilities) have shaped these initiatives. For example, case study 3.9 describes how the tax authority in Peru created an analytics unit (organizational capabilities) to develop predictive analytics about tax evasion (types and applications of analytics).

The case studies represent just a small portion of the diverse analytical work that public servants in the region have conducted within public administration. They were identified through a mixture of desk review and interviews with government officials and practitioners from multilateral organizations. Cases were then selected for inclusion in the report based on their potential to illustrate analytical concepts, policy objectives, challenges, and lessons. Each case study emphasizes evidence that is linked to the conceptual framework. However, not all elements of the conceptual framework are relevant to every case, so just the relevant evidence for selected elements and case studies is highlighted.

A reproducibility package is available for this book in the Reproducible Research Repository at https://reproducibility.worldbank.org/index.php/catalog/209.

The case studies demonstrate the wide variety of policy goals that can be pursued through government analytics. Analytics can inform decisions at different stages of program implementation: it can identify gaps and areas for improvements (for example, case study 3.2), test potential interventions before scale-up (for example, case study 3.6), and help define the implementation details of new policies (for example, case study 3.12). Analytical projects do not have to be complex to have an impact on policy making, but they do take time to mature and often develop through an iterative, trial-and-error approach. Governments should account for the time cycles associated with such an approach and nurture an enabling ecosystem to help analytical initiatives grow. In particular, dedicated analytics units and external collaborations can be effective strategies to leverage analytical capabilities. Connecting data from different information systems also enables data to be applied outside the government function that generated them, making a strong case for data accessibility across government organizations.

Finally, the 12 case studies presented in this chapter show that government analytics can be developed in any sector or ministry and at any level of government. There is no one-size-fits-all approach: a decentralized, ministry-specific analytics unit or a centralized, cross-cutting one can enable the use of data for analytics. The right approach to government analytics depends on context: policy-making challenges, decision-making needs, and strategic goals.

CASE STUDY 3.1: USING DESCRIPTIVE ANALYTICS TO REDUCE MISSED MEDICAL APPOINTMENTS (CHILE)

Missed appointments are a persistent problem for health care systems—and a costly one. In Chile, patients miss an estimated 10–20 percent of all scheduled appointments, resulting in an annual loss of approximately $180 million (Boone et al. 2022; CNEP 2022). Patients with chronic conditions that require continual monitoring and treatment—like hypertension and type 2 diabetes—are at particular risk if they miss appointments, which can increase mortality rates and health care costs.

To reduce missed medical appointments, Chile's Ministerio de Salud (Ministry of Health, or MINSAL) used descriptive analytics to better understand how missed appointments affect the country's health care system and develop a program in response. MINSAL drew on Chile's advanced health management information system (HealthMIS), which includes digital patient records with data about demographics, contact information, health visits, disease prevalence, and test results. In particular, MINSAL compared patient-level data on missed appointments with data on disease prevalence. By analyzing these data, MINSAL was able to better understand which patients missed appointments the most and formulate a policy tailored to this population's needs.

MINSAL discovered that patients with chronic conditions—approximately 60 percent of Chile's population (Margozzini and Passi 2018)—accounted for a significant fraction of missed appointments, and it responded by developing a program targeting them, the Mensajería para la Gestión de Citas en Pacientes Crónicos (Critical Care Appointment Management Program). Through this program, patients with chronic conditions received automated reminders by text message a few days before a scheduled appointment, with options to confirm, reschedule, or cancel the appointment. By encouraging patients to communicate with health clinics, the program aimed not just to reduce missed appointments but also to help clinics manage scheduling and allocate human resources more efficiently.

MINSAL's program effectively reduced missed appointments by 6 percent and increased the probability of using primary care services by 8.7 percent for patients with type 2 diabetes and by 10.7 percent for patients with hypertension (Boone et al. 2022, 2023; CNEP 2022). The program also improved health behaviors: it led patients to better adhere to prescribed medications and decreased in-hospital mortality rates.

In developing the program, MINSAL also discovered new information about the causes of missed appointments. While implementing the reminder system, MINSAL found missing and incorrect contact information in electronic records that accounted for about 20 percent of missed appointments (CNEP 2022). The discovery underscores the importance of implementing systematic data quality controls in information systems.

MINSAL's initiative illustrates the impact that relatively simple descriptive analytics can have when it is based on rich, comprehensive data (figure 3.1). By providing an accurate picture of health care challenges in Chile, descriptive analytics helped MINSAL pinpoint where problems were most acute and formulate a targeted policy to address them. It also revealed problems with the accuracy and completeness of the underlying data, enabling corrections to be made. In this way, MINSAL's program not only encouraged the patients who most need primary care services to use them but also strengthened the overall government analytics ecosystem in Chile.

FIGURE 3.1 Using Descriptive Analytics to Reduce Missed Medical Appointments, Chile

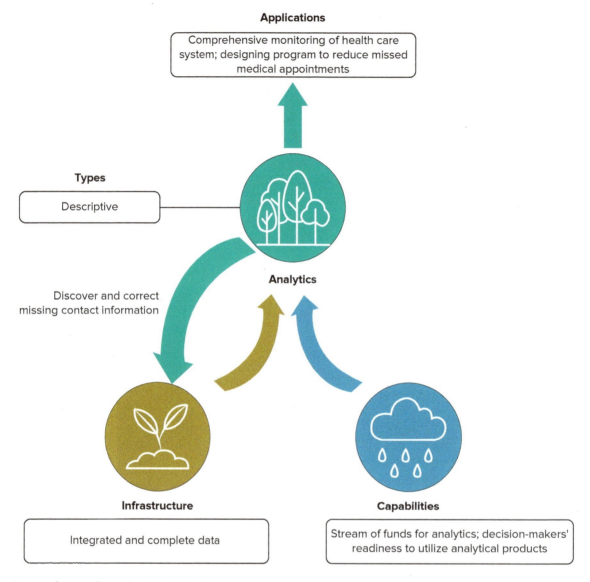

Source: Original figure for this publication.

CASE STUDY 3.2: USING DIAGNOSTIC ANALYTICS OF HUMAN RESOURCES DATA TO EXPLORE THE GENDER PAY GAP (COLOMBIA)

Colombia's Ley 1496/11 (Law 1496 of 2011) mandates that women and men receive equal pay and compensation for work of equal value. But is the law followed in practice?

The Unidad de Científicos de Datos (Data Scientists Unit, or UCD) of Colombia's Departamento Nacional de Planeación (National Planning Department) used a combination of descriptive and diagnostic analytics to determine whether there was a gender pay gap in the country among public sector workers with temporary contracts. Established in 2017, the UCD is a dedicated analytics unit that aims to harness the potential of administrative data to support the design, monitoring, and evaluation of public policies in Colombia.

To study pay differences among public sector workers, the UCD gained access to human resources management information system (HRMIS) data through data-sharing agreements with the Departamento Administrativo de la Función Pública (Administrative Department of the Public Service). The UCD used three data tables from the HRMIS that provided comprehensive information on public sector workers from 2012 to 2019, including the following:

- Personal information, such as name, gender, and date of birth (at the worker level)
- Education information (at the worker level)
- Information about the nature and financial value of contracts (at the contract level).

After integrating these data tables, the UCD conducted data quality checks to prepare the data for analytics. This involved eliminating duplicate entries, rectifying records with missing information or outliers, and resolving data validation errors.

The UCD began its study with descriptive analytics, by comparing average earnings between men and women across different years. This descriptive comparison offered valuable insights, but it did not account for other factors that might influence workers' pay, such as their work experience or education. To pinpoint the role of gender in pay differences, the UCD continued the study with diagnostic analytics. It used econometric models and hypothesis testing to compare workers who shared similar characteristics, including education, contract details, geographic region, and experience, isolating gender as the sole difference between them.

The UCD's study revealed a gender pay gap of 5–6 percent among temporary workers in the public sector (UCD 2019), and the National Planning Department informed the authorities that oversee gender policies of these findings. By combining different types of analytics, the UCD not only mapped pay differences among public sector workers (descriptive analytics) but also verified that gender accounted for part of those differences (diagnostic analytics). The UCD's analytical work demonstrates that good policy evaluation produces evidence describing not just *what* is happening but also *why* it is happening. It also offers an example of the critical role a dedicated analytics unit can play in generating that evidence and supporting better decision-making.

CASE STUDY 3.3: DATA ANALYTICS FOR CITIZEN ACCOUNTABILITY—THE CASE OF reACCIÓN (PARAGUAY)

In recent years, Paraguay has pledged to use revenue from electricity sales to fund local school infrastructure through the Fondo Nacional de Inversión Pública y Desarrollo (National Public Investment and Development Fund, or FONACIDE), established in 2012. However, as a result of local patronage and influence, funds have been channeled toward politically favored schools rather than the marginalized ones for which they were originally intended. In response, reAcción Paraguay, a recognized youth anticorruption organization, has analyzed open procurement data to ensure FONACIDE funds reach the intended schools, enhancing government transparency and strengthening citizen participation in the allocation of public resources (reAcción Paraguay, n.d.).

Paraguay has a rich legacy of data analytics in procurement and a resilient infrastructure for publishing open data. In addition to its efforts to make informed decisions based on timely, comprehensive analytics, the Dirección Nacional de Contrataciones Públicas (National Public Procurement Agency, or DNCP) has been committed to the recommendations of the Open Government Partnership since 2012. In 2014, the DNCP introduced a user-friendly, real-time open contracting portal with comprehensive information on tenders and contracts, machine-readable data, and an application programming interface for innovative data integration. Through this portal, Paraguay became the first country in the world to adopt the Open Contracting Data Standard for publication of and easy access to data on government contracts and public tenders (World Bank 2018).[1] The DNCP's commitment to publishing open data on public contracts has empowered journalists, activists, and civil society organizations to monitor public procurement and identify potential irregularities.

reAcción Paraguay has used the DNCP's open data portal to track the allocation of FONACIDE funds by developing a platform called FOCO that integrates these open procurement data with data from other official sources (like the Ministerio de Educación [Ministry of Education]) and data acquired during visits to schools (reAcción Paraguay 2023). FOCO had its start in a government-organized hackathon, a program to promote citizen-government interaction through technology (refer to other examples of this kind of initiative in case study 3.10). FOCO enables users to track infrastructure spending for eligible FONACIDE-funded schools by presenting data on the following:

- Infrastructure needs by year and school
- Schools' rankings on the Ministry of Education's priority list
- Schools that have received disbursements and the amounts of these disbursements

- Categories of spending that were covered by the disbursements (for example, classrooms, toilets, or furniture)
- Companies contracted for school improvements and the amounts of the contracts
- Results from inspections of target schools and FONACIDE-funded improvements.

FOCO has brought to light mismanagement of FONACIDE funds, increasing the fund's transparency and helping improve its administration, management, and integrity. For example, reAcción's monitoring led to a remarkable 400 percent increase in the accurate allocation of FONACIDE resources from 2015 to 2017 in Ciudad del Este, Paraguay's second-largest city (Riveros García 2019). As a result of reAcción's efforts, the DNCP was persuaded to reform FONACIDE's national procurement process. In 2020, reAcción began working directly with Paraguay's government to further develop data collection and analytics to make school infrastructure funding based on evidence a priority, and it continues to work with the DNCP and the Ministry of Education to monitor FONACIDE.

The example of reAcción Paraguay demonstrates that the impact of government analytics is amplified when data from different sources are connected. By building on open and accessible government data, a grassroots initiative was able to empower civic mobilization, help civil society uncover mismanagement of public funds, increase transparency and accountability, and improve the allocation of public resources.

CASE STUDY 3.4: BUILDING AN INTEGRATED HUMAN RESOURCES MANAGEMENT PLATFORM FOR STRATEGIC WORKFORCE PLANNING (URUGUAY)

Planning for the future of public administration requires data on the composition of the public sector workforce, the range of skills and competencies it encompasses, and future human capital requirements. The government of Uruguay and its Oficina Nacional del Servicio Civil (National Civil Service Office, or ONSC) are developing an innovative online platform for human resources management that makes these data available to public servants, policy makers, and the public to optimize the use of public resources; foster the enabling conditions for future analytics; and make government more open, transparent, and accountable to all (ONSC, n.d.).

The new platform is a collaborative effort that integrates and analyzes data from the information systems of multiple government organizations. As the organization leading this effort, the ONSC has been tasked with integrating, securing, and disseminating the data received from other organizations, including transforming the data to ensure they are consistent, comparable, accessible, and comprehensible to the public. The platform will introduce new features and descriptive analytics to provide timely, high-quality information to inform decision-making about public sector personnel, enhance recruitment, foster inclusivity in public employment for minority groups (including Afro-descendant people, people with disabilities, victims of violence, and transgender people), bolster government transparency and accountability, and streamline processes that support the rights and responsibilities of public workers.

To accomplish these goals, the platform will transform the landscape of public sector recruitment. One component, the "Digital CV," merges data from Uruguay Concursa, the existing public sector recruitment portal, with artificial intelligence to streamline recruitment, ensuring that public positions are filled with the most qualified candidates. The Digital CV will allow applicants and current employees to update information about their education, experience, career history, and skills for use in future selection processes. By providing a dynamic view of every job position and its holder—including each role's purpose, responsibilities, and skills—the Digital CV aims not just to improve recruitment but also to maintain a secure, organized database of jobs, systematically categorized by occupational categories, that can be used for strategic workforce planning and monitoring.

The platform will also enhance human resources management, especially performance evaluation. It will continuously update public servants' digital records with their achievements and competencies by integrating performance data. This will significantly reduce the time and effort involved in promotions and hiring. The platform will also enable users to view information about colleagues' and supervisors' performance, receive timely feedback, and set individual objectives, streamlining the talent management workflow.

Finally, the platform will provide analytics units, such as the ONSC's Laboratorio de Innovación y Observatorio de la Función Pública (Innovation Laboratory and Public Service Observatory), with a new source of integrated data. Among other things, analysts will be able to study the types of public servants who are poised to retire or move across positions, as well as the types of jobs the public administration has difficulty filling, to identify where extra resources will be essential for sustaining service delivery. For example, the Innovation Laboratory and Public Service Observatory has found that positions for specialized public servants are harder to fill than other types of positions and that the salary offered plays a crucial role in filling these positions (ONSC 2022a, 2022b, 2022c). From recruitment to human resources management to analytics, Uruguay's new platform demonstrates the impact government data can have when different administrative records are connected, the powerful applications that can be built using descriptive analytics techniques, and the importance of monitoring and analyzing the public sector workforce for strategic planning (figure 3.2).

FIGURE 3.2 Building an Integrated Human Resources Management Platform for Strategic Workforce Planning, Uruguay

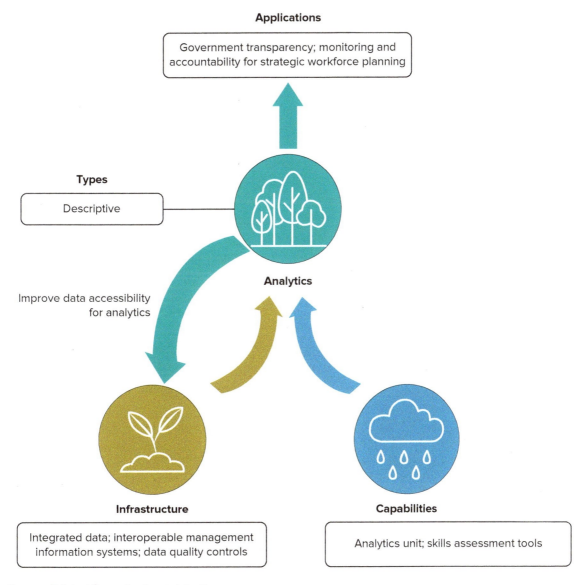

Source: Original figure for this publication.

CASE STUDY 3.5: ANALYZING TAX DATA TO INCREASE CORPORATE TAX COLLECTION (ECUADOR)

Tax evasion is a major concern for governments because it hampers tax collection and disrupts the allocation of resources within an economy. It can also lead to dependence on economically inefficient tax instruments. Traditionally, tax authorities have audited taxpayers to validate their declarations. Recently, they have also begun comparing their declarations with third-party data, such as employer-provided salary information or reports from firms' trading partners. This has become an essential tax collection strategy in high-income countries. Advancements in information technology and information systems have made third-party data more accessible and easier to use by integrating them with tax management information system (TaxMIS) data. These improvements hold promise for boosting tax collection efforts, especially in developing economies (Carrillo, Pomeranz, and Singhal 2017; Pomeranz and Vila-Belda 2019).

Ecuador's Servicio de Rentas Internas (Internal Revenue Service, or SRI), in collaboration with a team of researchers, evaluated the first systematic, large-scale application of third-party data to support Ecuador's tax enforcement efforts. Under this initiative, firms were notified when the revenue figures they had reported did not match third-party data from corporate tax returns detailing the value of their activities. Firms were urged to file amended returns based on the tax authority's access to these data.

To pinpoint discrepancies between the revenue figures reported by firms and those estimated by third parties, the SRI cross-referenced data from value added tax (VAT) return forms against multiple sources, including credit card sales, customs data, and financial institutions' records. The SRI's TaxMIS was instrumental in facilitating the efficient storage and retrieval of digital VAT information and corporate tax returns. The SRI's notifications to firms not only highlighted discrepancies in revenue between a firm's declaration and third-party data but also included the SRI's own revenue calculations.

Researchers estimated the effects of these notifications by analyzing changes in the firms' returns before and after receiving the notifications. They found that responding firms significantly adjusted their reported revenue, aligning it almost perfectly with the amount highlighted in the notifications. However, the researchers also found that firms adjusted reported costs, offsetting part of the potential increases in tax collection, which were estimated to be in the hundreds of millions of dollars annually. Understanding these responses is crucial for evaluating the effectiveness of third-party reporting, as its impact may be limited by enforcement constraints faced by tax authorities and offsetting adjustments made by taxpayers beyond just reported revenues.

Ecuador's initiative demonstrates that TaxMIS data (at the taxpayer or transaction level) can be useful beyond recording transactions. Tax authorities can also use these data to analyze taxpayer behavior, evaluate responses to policy and administration changes, and design optimal taxation policies (Brockmeyer 2019). More broadly, the initiative shows how administrative data can be used for rigorous policy evaluation, especially when multiple administrative records and nonadministrative databases are connected and external researchers and data analysts partner with public servants.

CASE STUDY 3.6: USING PREDICTIVE ANALYTICS TO PREVENT SCHOOL DROPOUTS (GUATEMALA)

Students who drop out of school earn less than peers who complete their education, and they face other socioeconomic challenges as well. Dropouts can be prevented through early warning systems that identify at-risk students and enable school staff members to take proactive measures and ensure success for all students. In Guatemala, where nearly 40 percent of sixth graders drop out of school before ninth grade, the Ministerio de Educación (Ministry of Education, or MINEDUC) has used analytics to build an effective early warning system (Haimovich, Vazquez, and Adelman 2021).

MINEDUC's analytics were enabled by the significant strides it has made in recent years to enhance its education management information system (EdMIS) and increase the availability of student-level data. These data—which concern families, attendance, and test scores—can be used to identify at-risk students. Importantly, MINEDUC also introduced unique student identifiers for all students in primary and secondary schools, which allow it to track the educational progress of Guatemalan students over time (Montes 2022).

In 2017, the government of Guatemala, in collaboration with the World Bank, developed the Estrategia Nacional para la Transición Exitosa (National Strategy for Successful Transition, or ENTRE), a program focusing on the transition from primary to lower secondary school. ENTRE used predictive analytics to develop an early warning system to identify students at risk of dropping out of school during this transition. MINEDUC leveraged student-level data from its EdMIS, linear regression models, and a simple algorithm to produce a list of students at risk of dropping out. After these students were identified, MINEDUC provided school principals with a list of students to target for additional support and offered teachers additional training in preventing dropouts. In its pilot phase, ENTRE was implemented in 4,000 public primary schools, representing 17 percent of Guatemala's primary schools.

ENTRE reduced the dropout rate in the transition from primary to lower secondary school by 9 percent within its first year, underscoring the program's effectiveness (Haimovich, Vazquez, and Adelman 2021). Moreover, ENTRE was designed to be scalable, since it could be implemented using primarily MINEDUC's existing administrative data structures, management systems, and personnel, with limited additional costs.

ENTRE illustrates how predictive analytics can offer a highly cost-effective method for building an early warning system to prevent dropouts, and the pilot has since been expanded into a nationwide program (MINEDUC 2019). By investing in the quality and availability of administrative data, Guatemala created the enabling conditions for applying predictive analytics, and by designing and implementing a program with analytics in mind, it was able to measure the program's effectiveness before scaling it up (figure 3.3).

FIGURE 3.3 Using Predictive Analytics to Prevent School Dropouts, Guatemala

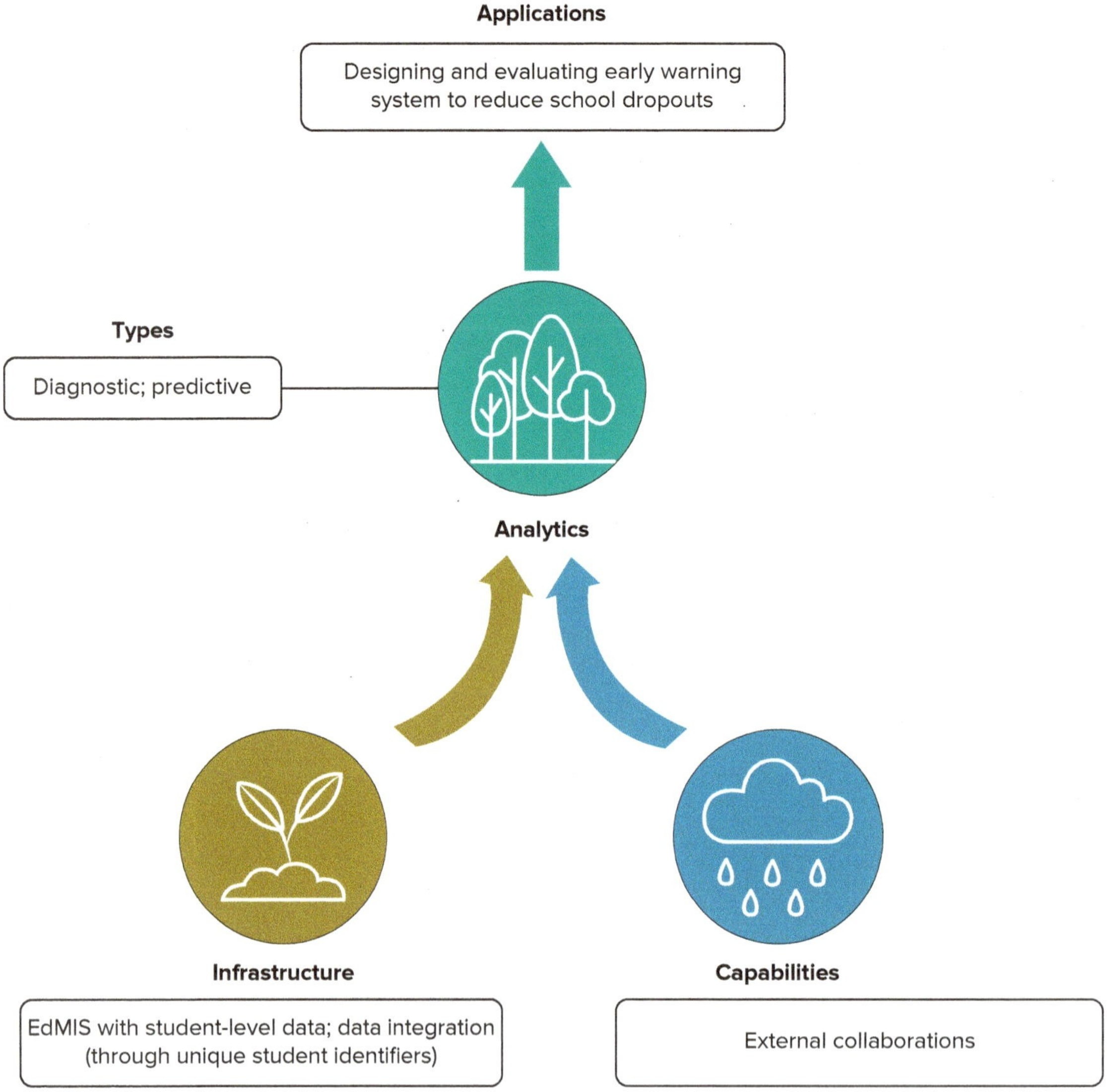

Applications

Designing and evaluating early warning system to reduce school dropouts

Types

Diagnostic; predictive

Analytics

Infrastructure

EdMIS with student-level data; data integration (through unique student identifiers)

Capabilities

External collaborations

Source: Original figure for this publication.
Note: EdMIS = education management information system.

CASE STUDY 3.7: USING TAX DATA TO BOOST PROCUREMENT EFFICIENCY (BRAZIL)

Public procurement can be made less efficient and less competitive by asymmetry of information between procurement officers and sellers. When procurement officers lack access to accurate market reference prices, their negotiating power is undermined, particularly in regard to products with limited providers. This can lead to higher purchase prices (Grennan and Swanson 2020). To address this challenge, the Secretaria da Fazenda do Estado do Rio Grande do Sul (Secretariat of Finance of the State of Rio Grande do Sul, or SEFAZ/RS) in Brazil introduced an innovative solution: a pricing algorithm that leverages electronic invoicing data from local business-to-business transactions to calculate market reference prices for pharmaceutical products.

To create this algorithm, SEFAZ/RS took advantage of existing data that had been integrated across data repositories. Since 2008, Brazil has required registered firms that are subject to state tax on the circulation of goods and services to issue digital invoices for their transactions. Over time, this transition to digital invoicing has produced a large body of transactions data. Although these transactions data were collected for taxation purposes, SEFAZ/RS saw that they could also be used to calculate market reference prices for procured products. If procurement officers had access to analytics based on these repurposed data, they would be better positioned to prepare tender documents and negotiate more competitive prices for products.

SEFAZ/RS designed an algorithm to guide the procurement of pharmaceutical products. The algorithm derived market reference prices from transactions data in three steps:

1. Identifying the product linked to a specific digital invoice
2. Breaking down the product into appropriate units for pricing
3. Calculating the reference price per unit.

In this way, SEFAZ/RS provided procurement officers with a price range for specific products derived from the distribution of past business-to-business transactions in the database.

When procurement officers were provided with market reference prices before they set tendering parameters, purchase prices were reduced (Martinez-Carrasco, Conceição, and Dezolt 2023). Products that had high initial unit prices, a limited number of suppliers, and a limited number of public buyers saw the most substantial price reductions. On average, the final prices of these products decreased by 13.2 percent, resulting in savings of approximately 4 percent on the average annual total expenditure for pharmaceutical products. Providing procurement officers with market reference prices thus appears to be an effective way to boost government efficiency in Brazil.

SEFAZ/RS's pricing algorithm demonstrates how data can be used for analytics across government functions. SEFAZ/RS conducted predictive analytics resulting in an analytical product that helps public servants do their jobs more effectively. By repurposing tax data, drawing on integrated data repositories, collaborating across units, and effectively integrating analytics into procurement officers' purchase process, SEFAZ/RS was able to establish a well-rooted analytics program with room to grow.

CASE STUDY 3.8: IMPROVING GOVERNMENT EFFICIENCY THROUGH A CENTRALIZED ANALYTICS UNIT (COLOMBIA)

At the end of the 2010s, Bogotá, Colombia, embarked on a journey to transform itself into a "smart city"—a city that is more sustainable, livable, and efficient for its inhabitants—by embracing smart technologies and data analytics. Guided by this vision, in 2020, the government of Bogotá established Ágata, a data analytics agency within the government (Alcaldía Mayor de Bogotá, Colombia 2020). Ágata is constituted as a simplified joint stock company in which different city government organizations and companies are partners. As a mixed-capital company, it funds its own operations, decreasing its reliance on public financing and the prevailing political will to advance data analytics.

Ágata functions as a centralized analytics unit for the city of Bogotá. It is responsible for generating insights across various information systems and government functions to address the needs of the city's stakeholders. With its current staff of 66 employees, Ágata produces an array of analytical products using descriptive, diagnostic, and predictive analytics, as well as artificial intelligence tools. Its centralized organizational model promotes economies of scale, allowing it to recruit employees with specialized analytical skills and develop a team with a holistic view of public administration, the challenges it faces, and the available data, reducing information silos. For the local government, the agency aims to improve decision-making by creating analytical products using data from multiple organizations. For citizens, it aims to elevate the quality of life, streamline access to public services, and promote the adoption and use of digital innovations.

From its inception, Ágata's analytical work has had an impact on diverse sectors, and the agency has expanded analytical capabilities in both the public and private sectors (Riaño and Delgado 2024). For example, Ágata played an important role during the COVID-19 pandemic by creating dashboards to track the spread of the virus across the city and monitor hospital occupancy rates. Using Ágata's analytics, the city could track changes in population mobility, design targeted interventions to stop the virus's spread, and ensure that the health care system could effectively manage its capacity. Ágata's work in the health sector has continued beyond the pandemic. Leveraging electronic health records and predictive analytics, it tracks pregnant women and newborns in real time to identify health risks. By encouraging preventive health measures, Ágata's analytics could save the lives of 870 newborns and 22 expectant mothers annually.

Ágata's projects have also had an impact on public financial management. For example, Ágata developed a platform that offers immediate access to comprehensive citizen data, including contact details and a record of services provided by the city (Riaño and Delgado 2024). By cleaning, standardizing, and integrating data from diverse sources, this platform aims to reduce the time government organizations need to prepare and use citizen data. By ensuring up-to-date contact information and cross-referencing each citizen's service and financial aid records, the platform aims to create efficiencies in resource allocation and reduce irregularities in service delivery.

Unless it makes proactive efforts to comprehend the needs of government organizations, a centralized analytics unit may become isolated from the broader structure and operations of public administration. This isolation can diminish the production and use of analytical products or make them less relevant and timely for decision-making. To mitigate this risk, Ágata conducts workshops with various organizations to understand their needs, assess how analytics could meet those needs, and determine which data could be used. It also hosts workshops with national government bodies and other local governments to expand its services and advance analytics throughout the public sector.

Ágata illustrates how a centralized analytics unit sustained by diverse sources of funding can advance the analytical journey of an entire government (figure 3.4). By addressing the demands of different government functions, from health to public finance, and by remaining responsive to the needs of policy makers, Ágata has dismantled information silos, enriching the Bogotá government's analytical perspective.

FIGURE 3.4 Improving Government Efficiency through a Centralized Analytics Unit, Colombia

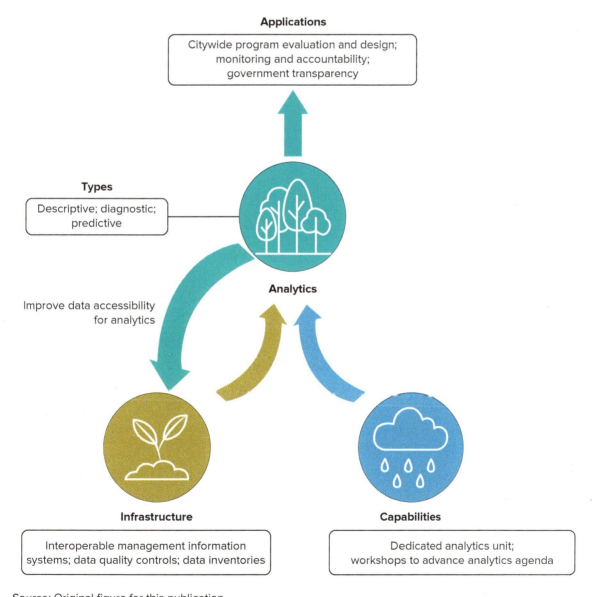

Source: Original figure for this publication.

CASE STUDY 3.9: ESTABLISHING A DECENTRALIZED ANALYTICS UNIT TO IMPROVE THE EFFICIENCY OF TAX COLLECTION (PERU)

Peru's fiscal situation deteriorated starting in 2014, with tax revenue decreasing from 18.2 percent of GDP (average 2005–14) to 16.4 percent of GDP (average 2015–21). These levels are below the average for Latin American and Caribbean countries (21.4 percent) and the member countries of the Organisation for Economic Co-operation and Development (33.5 percent) in the same period (2015–21). In addition to economic factors (such as a decline in mining prices and an economic slowdown in major trading partners), one factor contributing to the decrease in tax revenues was the difficulty faced by the Superintendencia Nacional de Aduanas y de Administración Tributaria (National Superintendency of Customs and Tax Administration, or SUNAT) in identifying tax evasion and underreporting of taxable activities (Luján Taipe and Sánchez Castro 2022).

SUNAT faced significant challenges in its effort to detect tax evasion and improve tax reporting. Traditional processes were complex and slow, and the systems and databases required technological upgrades to meet current needs. To address these challenges, since 2019, SUNAT has initiated a strategic transformation—including creating a dedicated analytics unit—to better understand and predict taxpayer behavior.

SUNAT's application of data analytics is part of a broader set of reforms to digitalize revenue collection, improve efficiency, and foster a more user-friendly approach. SUNAT improved taxpayer services by reviewing and simplifying responses to their inquiries and streamlined the processing of electronic invoices to provide timely access to transactional data (enhancing voluntary tax compliance). It also developed and automated its TaxMIS, applying a set of detailed definitions and specifications for cross-referencing information using key information sources such as electronic purchase records, electronic sales records, electronic payment receipts, and tax forms. These broader reforms enabled analysis based on TaxMIS data.

In 2019, SUNAT established a dedicated analytics unit to enhance tax and customs control and compliance. The unit consisted of five data scientists who developed analytics to detect evasion and optimize audits using TaxMIS data in combination with external data sources. Among the first projects developed by the unit to improve tax compliance were the following:

- Using big data techniques such as web scraping, the unit developed an algorithm to determine whether e-commerce sellers were registered in the taxpayer registry and discovered that 57 percent were not. SUNAT sent a text message to these sellers, resulting in the registration of 320 new sellers and an increase of about $1 million in sales declarations.

- Using text mining, the unit developed an automated alert system to prevent taxpayers from deducting expenses unrelated to their business. The unit's analysis revealed that, on average, taxpayers did not record 64 out of every 100 invoices that the alert system had flagged as personal expenses, protecting them from fines and audits.

- The unit developed a taxpayer segmentation model to help SUNAT focus its collection strategies (Larios, Azuero, and Rojas 2018; SUNAT 2019).

Since 2019, the analytics unit has continued to grow and to develop new predictive analytics to help SUNAT assess the risk of tax noncompliance. For example, the unit developed a model to determine the risk that taxpayers lack the operational capacity to carry out a declared economic activity, helping to prevent the generation of improper tax credits or deductible expenses. This model has generated $15 million, and SUNAT has scheduled operational capacity verifications with 1,780 taxpayers flagged by the model. The unit also developed a model to optimize the allocation of SUNAT's resources that identifies high-risk taxpayers and assigns them a priority level based on the unit's operational capacity and the probability and impact of noncompliance (SUNAT 2022). These models have become substantial components of risk management at SUNAT.

SUNAT's strategic transformation demonstrates the impact that a dedicated analytics unit can have within an organization, especially when analytics is part of a broader reform strategy. By producing analytics closely aligned with operational needs, SUNAT's analytics unit has supported the agency's transformation and Peru's fiscal sustainability.

CASE STUDY 3.10: DATATHONS AS A TOOL FOR PROMOTING DATA ANALYTICS (MULTIPLE COUNTRIES)

In recent years, "datathons" have become an important tool within the data science community for promoting the use of analytics and encouraging the sharing of best practices, tools, and success stories. This type of event has recently gained traction in the public sector. At a public sector datathon, public servants and members of the public are given access to government data, learn about a relevant policy question, and collaborate to produce analytics that can be used to inform policy making. Participants work to uncover patterns and trends in the data, demonstrating how analytics can be used to conceptualize or address problems.

Public sector datathons can benefit governments even beyond the analytical insights produced during the events. When datathons are open to both public servants and the wider community, they help governments discover analytical talent, creating a pool of candidates for future recruitment. Datathons also engage individuals with diverse skills to tackle policy challenges in a collaborative and informal environment, which can foster the development of innovative ideas and encourage participants to apply their newfound insights within their own workplaces. Moreover, datathons signal an organizational commitment to analytics, which can make public sector data analysts more satisfied with their jobs and improve retention.

Numerous countries in Latin America and the Caribbean have adopted datathons as a strategy to encourage analytical experimentation. For instance, in 2022, Ecuador's Servicio

Nacional de Contratación Pública (National Public Procurement Service) organized a datathon, Rompiendo la Contratación Pública (Disrupting Public Procurement), to discover innovative applications of data from the e-Procurement system (SERCOP 2022). The event, which spanned four days, was open to both public servants and the public. Participants developed analytical products, including interactive visualizations and statistical models, to understand the factors influencing local purchasing, the role of public procurement in boosting the local economy, and sectors lacking gender diversity among suppliers. They also devised alert systems to flag conflicts of interest in public purchases.

Similarly, in 2023, Mexico's Secretaría Ejecutiva del Sistema Nacional Anticorrupción (Executive Secretariat of the National Anti-Corruption System) organized a datathon focused on applying data in the fight against corruption. Participants were encouraged to develop algorithms using e-Procurement data to detect behavioral patterns associated with administrative misconduct among public officials and private organizations, including improper hiring practices, influence peddling, and collusion in procurement (SESNA 2023).

In Brazil, meanwhile, the Escola Nacional de Administração Pública (National School of Public Administration) organized a datathon focused on studying racial inequalities in the public service. Leveraging HRMIS data, participating teams studied the areas of public policy where Black public servants are employed, the dynamics affecting the appointment of Black people into leadership roles in the public service, and the main barriers to Black people's access to public service positions (ENAP 2023).

As these examples show, datathons represent a valuable tool for fostering the development of analytical products across different government functions. They provide a platform through which both public servants and external experts can share and learn best practices, cultivate talent, and build up organizational identification and commitment. Datathons also highlight the significance of government analytics for identifying issues within public administration and proposing solutions, showcasing the need for more and better analytics to improve public policy.

CASE STUDY 3.11: THE POWER OF DATA INTEGRATION TO STRENGTHEN THE INTEGRITY OF PUBLIC PROCUREMENT (BRAZIL)

Corruption significantly undermines development, and public procurement is exceptionally vulnerable, leading to considerable waste of public resources. Corruption represents an estimated 8 percent of the global value of procurement contracts, reaching some $880 billion lost yearly (Bosio 2021), and current methods for detecting and investigating corruption in procurement are insufficient relative to the problem's vast scale. Approaches that rely on manual analysis, follow-up investigations of specific complaints, and anecdotal evidence are inefficient, because they demand extensive human and financial resources. But advancements in data collection, digitalization, and transparency within the public sector have paved the way for data-driven anticorruption strategies.

In this context, the World Bank, in partnership with subnational governments in Brazil, developed the Governance Risk Assessment System (GRAS). This cutting-edge tool harnesses analytics to detect fraud, corruption, and collusion in public procurement. GRAS uses algorithms to identify risk patterns associated with public procurement fraud and corruption, targeting public suppliers, contracting agencies, and individual actors. A pillar of GRAS is its robust data integration framework, which aggregates, links, and analyzes large volumes of public procurement data, including detailed microdata on firms and individuals (World Bank 2023). This integration framework makes it easier to identify risk patterns that could not be identified by analyzing a single data set.

GRAS encompasses 60 red flags and examines risk patterns across four dimensions. The first dimension focuses on the procurement cycle, and GRAS flags tendering processes that lack public announcements or in which a single bid is submitted. The second focuses on interbidder collusion, such as that which can occur when competitors have a common shareholder or their behavior suggests coordinated bidding. The third focuses on supplier characteristics, including registration in tax haven jurisdictions, unusually high profitability, and engaging in multiple economic activities. Finally, the fourth dimension focuses on the political connections of suppliers, such as those implied by their contributions to electoral campaigns or political parties and by their having public officials or politicians as shareholders.

In 2022, the World Bank piloted GRAS in the states of Mato Grosso and Rio de Janeiro and the municipalities of São Paulo and Porto Alegre. During the pilot, GRAS identified about 800 firms that had been awarded contracts despite being under legal sanctions, about 4,000 firms that had been awarded contracts despite being owned by public servants or having other political connections, and about 1,000 firms that had won bids against competitors with a common shareholder (World Bank 2023). During the pilot, GRAS also supported corruption investigations by public prosecutors' offices. In one participating state, GRAS-supported analyses helped the federal police uncover networks of shell companies and a money-laundering operation (World Bank 2023).

These findings underscore the pervasive risks of corruption and conflicts of interest within public procurement. GRAS demonstrates how public sector corruption can be detected and reduced by integrating government data, applying descriptive and predictive analytics, and triangulating data, presenting a promising model for using analytics to foster integrity and transparency in public procurement.

CASE STUDY 3.12: SUPPORTING THE IMPLEMENTATION OF FRAMEWORK AGREEMENTS THROUGH DATA ANALYTICS (URUGUAY)

Public procurement covers diverse purchases, and the best purchasing strategies vary across different categories of product. One purchasing strategy is to establish *framework agreements*, umbrella agreements that establish the terms—including price, quality, and quantity—under which purchasing organizations can award contracts for a specific product to preapproved suppliers. For example, a country's central procurement unit might establish a framework agreement with an information technology company to purchase computers for the country's entire public administration for five years. Framework agreements are efficient purchasing strategies for products that represent low supply risks and that are purchased in large quantities and across many procuring organizations. Analytics can help define efficient purchasing strategies for different products, including by helping prepare framework agreements.

In 2019, a World Bank review of Uruguay's public procurement data identified consolidation of purchases as the most significant potential source of savings and pointed to framework agreements as the most effective instrument for implementing the required strategy (Cocciolo, Samaddar, and Fazekas 2023).[2] Procurement regulations in Uruguay already covered the use of framework agreements for common goods and services, making framework agreements an easy strategy to implement without changes in laws and regulations. In 2021, the World Bank worked with Uruguay's Agencia Reguladora de Compras Estatales (Regulatory Agency for Public Procurement) and the Unidad Centralizada de Adquisiciones (Central Procurement Unit) within the Ministry of Economy and Finance to build the organizations' capacity to generate and manage framework agreements and develop pilot framework agreements for goods and services with the greatest savings potential (Cocciolo, Samaddar, and Fazekas 2023).

During this review's implementation phase, analytics was useful for identifying items that could be purchased through framework agreements. With the support of the World Bank, the agency developed an algorithm that considers the total procurement volume of a product per year, the number of procuring organizations purchasing it, and the number of purchases and procurement procedures per year. The algorithm has been useful for identifying and giving priority to sectors and products with the largest potential for efficiency gains and for targeting the next steps in the preparation of framework agreements (for example, consolidation of purchases and market analysis). Uruguay's experience demonstrates the impact of descriptive and diagnostic analytics for identifying suitable interventions and supporting their design during the implementation stage of a program.

NOTES

1. More information about the standard can be found on the website of the Open Contracting Partnership at https://standard.open-contracting.org/latest/en/.
2. "Consolidation of purchases" refers to the practice of grouping purchases of the same product or service to reduce duplication. Purchases can be consolidated within one procuring organization or across procuring organizations by aggregating fragmented purchases into larger contracts. The goal is to improve efficiency by streamlining procurement processes, reducing procedural costs, stimulating competition, and exploiting economies of scale.

REFERENCES

Alcaldía Mayor de Bogotá, Colombia. 2020. "Ágata, la nueva agencia analítica de datos que hará de Bogotá líder global en transparencia e inteligencia digital para sus ciudadanos." Noticias, December 14, 2020. https://www.sdp.gov.co/noticias/agata-la-nueva-agencia-analitica-de-datos-hara-de-bogota-lider-global-transparencia-e-inteligencia.

Boone, Claire E., Pablo Celhay, Paul Gertler, and Tadeja Gracner. 2023. "Encouraging Preventative Care to Manage Chronic Disease at Scale." NBER Working Paper 31643, National Bureau of Economic Research, Cambridge, MA. https://doi.org/10.3386/w31643.

Boone, Claire E., Pablo Celhay, Paul Gertler, Tadeja Gracner, and Josefina Rodriguez. 2022. "How Scheduling Systems with Automated Appointment Reminders Improve Health Clinic Efficiency." *Journal of Health Economics* 82: 102598. https://doi.org/10.1016/j.jhealeco.2022.102598.

Bosio, Erica. 2021. "Reducing Corruption in Public Procurement." *Let's Talk Development* (blog), August 17, 2021. https://blogs.worldbank.org/en/developmenttalk/reducing-corruption-public-procurement.

Brockmeyer, Anne. 2019. "Working with Administrative Tax Data: A How-to-Get-Started Guide." Macroeconomics, Trade & Investment (MTI) Practice Note 7, World Bank, Washington, DC. https://www.annebrockmeyer.com/uploads/1/2/1/4/121485108/mti_practice_note_on_admin_tax_data.pdf.

Carrillo, Paul, Dina Pomeranz, and Monica Singhal. 2017. "Dodging the Taxman: Firm Misreporting and Limits to Tax Enforcement." *American Economic Journal: Applied Economics* 9 (2): 144–64. https://doi.org/10.1257/app.20140495.

CNEP (Comisión Nacional de Evaluación y Productividad). 2022. *Eficiencia en la Gestión de Atención Primaria de Salud (APS)*. Santiago, Chile: Comisión Nacional de Evaluación y Productividad. https://cnep.cl/estudios-finalizados/eficiencia-en-gestion-de-atencion-primaria-de-la-salud/.

Cocciolo, Serena, Suxhmita Samaddar, and Mihaly Fazekas. 2023. "Government Analytics Using Procurement Data." In *The Government Analytics Handbook: Leveraging Data to Strengthen Public Administration*, edited by Daniel Rogger and Christian Schuster, chap. 12. Washington, DC: World Bank. https://doi.org/10.1596/978-1-4648-1957-5.

ENAP (Escola Nacional de Administração Pública). 2023. "DATATHON Desigualdades Raciais no Serviço Público." Notice 119/2023, Process 04600.002764/2023-26, Brasília, Brazil. https://repositorio.enap.gov.br/bitstream/1/7779/1/Edital%20Datathon%20Desigualdades%20Raciais.pdf.

Grennan, Matthew, and Ashley Swanson. 2020. "Transparency and Negotiated Prices: The Value of Information in Hospital-Supplier Bargaining." *Journal of Political Economy* 128 (4): 1234–68. https://doi.org/10.1086/705329.

Haimovich, Francisco, Emmanuel Vazquez, and Melissa Adelman. 2021. "Scalable Early Warning Systems for School Dropout Prevention: Evidence from a 4,000-School Randomized Controlled Trial." Policy Research Working Paper 9685, World Bank, Washington, DC. https://documents.worldbank.org/en/publication/documents-reports/documentdetail/983591622568486300/scalable-early-warning-systems-for-school-dropout-prevention-evidence-from-a-4-000-school-randomized-controlled-trial

Larios, José, Rodrigo Azuero, and Agnes Rojas. 2018. "Utilizando big data para combatir la evasión." *Recaudando Bienestar* (blog), August 29, 2018. https://blogs.iadb.org/gestion-fiscal/es/utilizando-big-data-para-combatir-la-evasion/.

Luján Taipe, Jhonatan Erick, and Lucía Carmen Sánchez Castro. 2022. "Implementando la Transformación Digital en SUNAT: acercándonos al contribuyente." MBA thesis, Universidad de Piura. https://hdl.handle.net/11042/5525.

Margozzini, Paula, and Álvaro Passi. 2018. "Encuesta Nacional de Salud, ENS 2016–2017: Un aporte a la planificación sanitaria y políticas públicas en Chile." *Ars Medica: Revista de Ciencias Médicas* 43 (1): 30–34. https://doi.org/10.11565/arsmed.v43i1.1354.

Martinez-Carrasco, Jose, Otavia Conceição, and Ana Luzia Dezolt. 2023. "More Information, Lower Price? Access to Market-Based Reference Prices and Gains in Public Procurement Efficiency." Working Paper IDB-WP-1441, Inter-American Development Bank, Washington, DC. http://dx.doi.org/10.18235/0004794.

MINEDUC (Ministerio de Educación [de Guatemala]). 2019. *Guía para promover la transición exitosa de sexto primaria a primer grado del ciclo básico*. 2nd ed. Guatemala City: MINEDUC. https://cnbguatemala.org/wiki/Gu%C3%ADa_para_promover_la_transici%C3%B3n_exitosa_de_sexto_Primaria_a_primer_grado_del_Ciclo_B%C3%A1sico.

Montes, Nancy. 2022. *Usos de los sistemas de información en el planeamiento y gestión de políticas educativas en América Latina: Informe regional*. Buenos Aires, Argentina: Oficina para América Latina y el Caribe del Instituto Internacional de Planeamiento de la Educación de la Organización de las Naciones Unidas para la Educación, la Ciencia y la Cultura. https://unesdoc.unesco.org/ark:/48223/pf0000385439.locale=en.

ONSC (Oficina Nacional del Servicio Civil). 2022a. "Análisis de los concursos desiertos de la Administración Central, 2011–2022." Documento de Trabajo 03/2022. ONSC, Montevideo, Uruguay. https://www.gub.uy/oficina-nacional-servicio-civil/comunicacion/publicaciones/analisis-concursos-desiertos-administracion-central-2011-2022.

ONSC (Oficina Nacional del Servicio Civil). 2022b. "Avances en la Plataforma de Gestión Humana del Estado." Noticias, August 4, 2022. ONSC, Montevideo, Uruguay. https://www.gub.uy/oficina-nacional-servicio-civil/comunicacion/noticias/avances-plataforma-gestion-humana-del-estado.

ONSC (Oficina Nacional del Servicio Civil). 2022c. "Nueva Plataforma de Gestión Humana del Estado GHE.uy." ONSC tv. Streamed live on November 23, 2022. YouTube video, 1:05:25. https://www.youtube.com/watch?v=u51tU2mxR_E.

ONSC (Oficina Nacional del Servicio Civil). n.d. "Proyecto estratégico: Plataforma de Gestión Humana del Estado (ghe.uy)." Accessed February 28, 2024. https://www.gub.uy/oficina-nacional-servicio-civil/politicas-y-gestion/proyectos/plataforma-gestion-humana-del-estado-gheuy.

Pomeranz, Dina, and José Vila-Belda. 2019. "Taking State-Capacity Research to the Field: Insights from Collaborations with Tax Authorities." *Annual Review of Economics* 11: 755–81. https://doi.org/10.1146/annurev-economics-080218-030312.

reAcción Paraguay. 2023. "FOCO." Last modified February 19, 2023. https://foco.reaccion.org.py/.

reAcción Paraguay. n.d. "reAcción." Accessed July 17, 2024. https://reaccion.org.py/.

Riaño, Manuel, and Alejandro Delgado. 2024. *Yo, IA Innovación gubernamental: La era de la inteligencia artificial*. Barcelona: Bronce.

Riveros García, David. 2019. "Politics, Technology, and Accountability: The Transparency Façade of Open Government Data Reforms in Paraguay." *eJournal of eDemocracy and Open Government* (JeDEM) 11 (2): 60–93. https://doi.org/10.29379/jedem.v11i2.537.

SERCOP (Servicio Nacional de Contratación Pública). 2022. "Datatón–Rompiendo la Contratación Pública." SERCOP, Quito, Ecuador. https://dataton.compraspublicas.gob.ec/wp-content/uploads/2022/04/Metodologia-Evento-Dataton_vf-2.pdf.

SESNA (Secretaría Ejecutiva del Sistema Nacional Anticorrupción). 2023. "Datatón Anticorrupción 2023: Convocatoria." SESNA, Mexico City. https://dataton2023.plataformadigitalnacional.org/files/datatonanticorrupcion2023-basesv1_3.pdf.

SUNAT (Superintendencia Nacional de Aduanas y de Administración Tributaria). 2019. "Memoria Anual 2019: Resumen Ejecutivo." SUNAT, Lima, Peru. https://www.sunat.gob.pe/cuentassunat/planestrategico/memoria/ejecutiva/memoriaEje-2019.pdf.

SUNAT (Superintendencia Nacional de Aduanas y de Administración Tributaria). 2022. *Memoria Institucional 2022*. Lima, Peru: SUNAT. https://www.sunat.gob.pe/cuentassunat/planestrategico/memoria/memoria2022.pdf.

UCD (Unidad de Científicos de Datos). 2019. "Dirección de Desarrollo Digital." Departamento Nacional de Planeación, Bogotá, Colombia. https://colaboracion.dnp.gov.co/CDT/Desarrollo%20Digital/UCD/Proyectos/2019_24_Brecha_salarial/Brecha_salarial_Informe.pdf.

World Bank. 2018. "Paraguay: Systematic Country Diagnostic." World Bank, Washington, DC. https://documents1.worldbank.org/curated/en/827731530819395899/pdf/Paraguay-SCD-06292018.pdf.

World Bank. 2023. *Governance Risk Assessment System (GRAS): Advanced Data Analytics for Detecting Fraud, Corruption, and Collusion in Public Expenditures*. Equitable Growth, Finance and Institutions Insight—Governance. Washington, DC: World Bank. https://openknowledge.worldbank.org/handle/10986/40640.

CHAPTER 4

A Regional Assessment of Government Analytics in Latin America and the Caribbean

INTRODUCTION

This chapter offers a comprehensive assessment of government analytics and its enabling conditions in Latin America and the Caribbean, based on data from an original survey conducted in 20 countries (map 4.1). In each country, public servants who are experts in core government functions and their respective management information systems (MISs) were interviewed, making it possible to assess how different kinds of administrative data are used to address policy-making challenges. For this reason, most of the analysis is presented at the information system level.[1] The survey targeted MISs associated with core government functions: education (education management information system, or EdMIS), health (health management information system, or HealthMIS), human resources (human resources management information system, or HRMIS), procurement (e-Procurement), public finance (public financial management information system, or PFMIS), and taxation (tax management information system, or TaxMIS). Country-level data on government initiatives for cultivating the analytical capabilities of public servants were also collected. Survey data are analyzed according to the conceptual framework introduced in chapter 2: first, the chapter describes what government analytics looks like in the region, then it analyzes governments' organizational and individual capabilities, as well as their data infrastructures.

The regional assessment highlights the ways governments across Latin America and the Caribbean are already leveraging administrative data for analytics as well as policy areas where analytics can help address further challenges. It shows that governments in the region predominantly use administrative data to produce descriptive analytics for operational and transactional purposes, like monitoring and accountability. This means governments are missing out on opportunities to use advanced analytics to improve decision-making, design more effective and efficient public policies, and strengthen public sector functioning and service delivery.

A reproducibility package is available for this book in the Reproducible Research Repository at https://reproducibility.worldbank.org/index.php/catalog/209.

MAP 4.1 Countries in Latin America and the Caribbean That Participated in the Survey

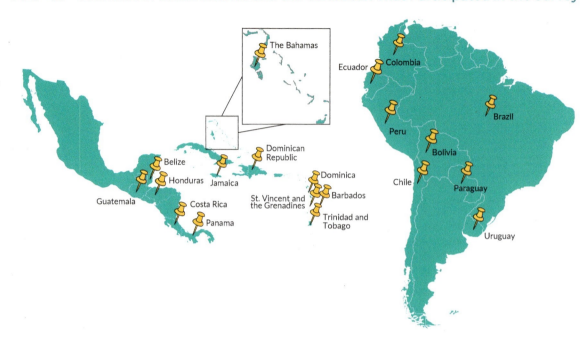

Source: Original map for this publication.

Strengthening the enabling conditions for government analytics is key to capitalizing on these opportunities. For now, governments in Latin America and the Caribbean face significant challenges in building analytical capabilities within government organizations. Although they acknowledge the importance of analytical skills and in some cases offer training programs for analytics, governments lack structured career tracks for data analysts, proficiency evaluations on data analytics for public servants, funding for analytical projects, and an overall strategy for moving public administration toward evidence-based policy making. But some governments are also pursuing two promising strategies for addressing limited analytical capabilities: collaborating with academic or international organizations and establishing dedicated analytics units.

Governments in the region also face data infrastructure challenges that prevent them from fully unlocking the transformative potential of digital MISs and catalyzing the value of the investments they have already made. As the case studies in chapter 3 demonstrate, analytics can have the biggest impact on policy making when government data from different sources are combined. Despite the progress they have made in digitalization, many governments in the region still contend with MISs that are limited in data comprehensiveness and functionality, fragmented systems, informal data access protocols, and limited quality control measures. Governments need to improve the functionality, interoperability, and data quality of MISs so these systems can better support informed decision-making.

Finally, the regional assessment reveals that analytics, capabilities, and infrastructure vary significantly, not only across countries but also across government functions, suggesting that governments lack a systematic approach to analytics for the whole of public administration. Although analytical products have the greatest impact when they respond to specific policy needs, governments can avoid fragmented and duplicated efforts by developing government-wide enabling ecosystems for analytics. As the survey results show, this kind of approach is especially needed to ensure the interoperability of MISs, build analytical capabilities, and create a culture for evidence-based decision-making in public administration. By breaking down how the different elements of the conceptual framework vary across MISs, this chapter offers evidence to help governments identify opportunities and weaknesses for themselves and determine how to develop enabling ecosystems within their administrations.

> **Throughout this chapter, the voices of the public servant experts that were surveyed are highlighted in blue speech bubbles like this one.**

SURVEY METHODOLOGY

As noted earlier, the Government Analytics Survey in Latin America and the Caribbean was conducted in 20 countries. It consisted of seven questionnaires (presented in online appendix D). Six individual MIS-level questionnaires focused separately on each type of MIS (EdMIS, HealthMIS, HRMIS, e-Procurement, PFMIS, and TaxMIS). One additional country-level questionnaire, the "capabilities questionnaire," focused on government initiatives for cultivating the analytical capabilities of public servants. More than 100 government officials responded to the questionnaires, providing insights based on their specific areas of expertise.

The capabilities questionnaire was typically completed by the country's digital government agency ($n = 16$ countries). MIS questionnaires were completed by different public sector organizations, depending on the government function involved. The EdMIS questionnaire was typically completed by the country's ministry of education ($n = 13$ countries), the e-Procurement questionnaire by the country's procurement agency ($n = 11$ countries), the HealthMIS questionnaire by the ministry of health ($n = 14$ countries), the HRMIS questionnaire by the ministry of civil service ($n = 14$ countries), the PFMIS questionnaire by the ministry of finance or economy ($n = 16$ countries), and the TaxMIS questionnaire by the government's tax authority ($n = 17$ countries). For further information on the survey methodology, refer to appendix A.

WHAT DOES GOVERNMENT ANALYTICS LOOK LIKE IN LATIN AMERICA AND THE CARIBBEAN?

What Types of Analytics Do Governments Conduct?

Governments in Latin America and the Caribbean primarily use administrative data for descriptive analytics. In the region, 96 percent of MISs are used for descriptive analytics, and this trend is consistent across all the government functions considered in the survey (figure 4.1). As noted in the conceptual framework in chapter 2, descriptive analytics allows government organizations to understand the current state of their operations and summarize data for tracking and reporting. Diagnostic analytics is the second-most-used type of analytics (55 percent of MISs) in the region, and predictive analytics is employed a little less often (50 percent of MISs).

FIGURE 4.1 Types of Analytics, by Type of MIS

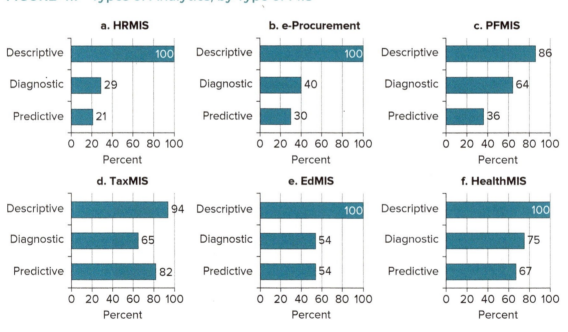

Source: Government Analytics Survey in Latin America and the Caribbean.
Note: The figure shows, by type of MIS, the proportion of systems in the region used for each type of analytics. The results for each type of MIS do not total 100 percent because the question allowed for multiple responses. N = 85 country-MISs, distributed as follows: EdMIS questionnaire (n = 13 countries); e-Procurement questionnaire (n = 11 countries); HealthMIS questionnaire (n = 14 countries); HRMIS questionnaire (n = 14 countries); PFMIS questionnaire (n = 16 countries); TaxMIS questionnaire (n = 17 countries). EdMIS = education management information system; e-Procurement = procurement management information system; HealthMIS = health management information system; HRMIS = human resources management information system; MIS = management information system; PFMIS = public financial management information system; TaxMIS = tax management information system.

> "Efforts are being made to incorporate predictive models in health care; however, the main problem is that there are no systems in place to generate these models."
>
> – HealthMIS expert

The types of analytics governments undertake differ across MISs and among countries. Descriptive analytics is the most common, as illustrated in figure 4.2. Diagnostic analytics alone is the least common: only in one country is the PFMIS used for diagnostic analytics alone. Data from TaxMISs, EdMISs, and HealthMISs are used for more complex types of analytics (combinations of descriptive, diagnostic, and predictive analytics) in numerous countries, suggesting a more sophisticated approach to analytics in these government functions. For example, predictive analytics most often draws on tax data (primarily to generate tax revenue forecasts) and health data (for instance, to predict the likelihood of disease spread and support planning for prevention campaigns). Data from HRMISs, on the other hand, are primarily used for less complex descriptive analytics. These patterns suggest that governments in the region do not yet use their administrative data and analytics tools to their full potential. More steps can be taken to use administrative data, especially those from HRMISs, PFMISs, and e-Procurement systems, for strategic applications based on diagnostic and predictive analytics: for instance, to identify the root causes of performance gaps, support forecasting, and inform policy design.

FIGURE 4.2 Types of Analytics, by Country and Type of MIS

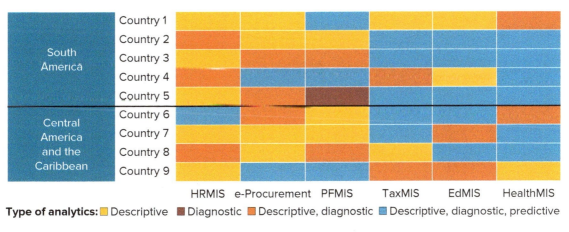

Source: Government Analytics Survey in Latin America and the Caribbean.
Note: The figure shows the types of analytics conducted across MISs and countries in the region. The data presented include only countries that completed all six MIS questionnaires. *N* = 54 country-MISs. EdMIS = education management information system; e-Procurement = procurement management information system; HealthMIS = health management information system; HRMIS = human resources management information system; MIS = management information system; PFMIS = public financial management information system; TaxMIS = tax management information system.

Just as not all MISs are used for all types of analytics, not all data elements within MISs are used equally. Although most available data within each type of MIS seem to be used for some type of analytics, the specific data elements that are used vary, and distinct patterns emerge across each type of MIS (figure 4.3). For instance, within HRMISs, data on employment status and personnel characteristics are extensively

FIGURE 4.3 Data Elements Used for Analytics, by Type of MIS

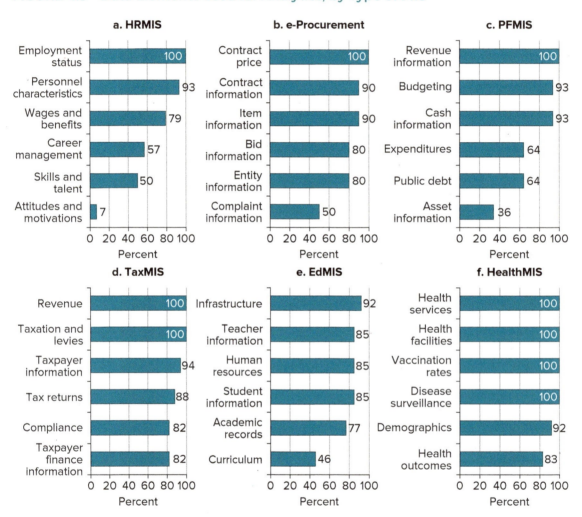

Source: Government Analytics Survey in Latin America and the Caribbean.
Note: The figure shows, by type of MIS, the proportion of systems in the region that uses each type of data element for analytics. The data presented include only countries with the specified data elements in their MISs. The results for each type of MIS do not total 100 percent because the question allowed for multiple responses. $N = 85$ country-MISs, distributed as follows: EdMIS questionnaire ($n = 13$ countries); e-Procurement questionnaire ($n = 11$ countries); HealthMIS questionnaire ($n = 14$ countries); HRMIS questionnaire ($n = 14$ countries); PFMIS questionnaire ($n = 16$ countries); TaxMIS questionnaire ($n = 17$ countries). EdMIS = education management information system; e-Procurement = procurement management information system; HealthMIS = health management information system; HRMIS = human resources management information system; MIS = management information system; PFMIS = public financial management information system; TaxMIS = tax management information system.

> "Although we cover the six data elements described, it should be clarified that they are found in different systems."
>
> – EdMIS expert

used for analytics (100 and 93 percent of HRMISs, respectively), mainly for reporting purposes. Data on employees' skills and talents and on their attitudes and motivations are comparatively underutilized (50 and 7 percent of HRMISs, respectively). Likewise, within e-Procurement systems, data on complaints are the least used (50 percent of e-Procurement systems), whereas data on contract prices are extensively used (100 percent of e-Procurement systems). Within PFMISs, data on state-owned assets are highly underutilized for analytics (36 percent of PFMISs), whereas revenue information and budgeting data are extensively used (100 percent and 93 percent of PFMISs, respectively). Finally, within EdMISs, curriculum data and students' academic records are the least used for analytics (46 and 77 percent of EdMISs, respectively).

Why do governments use some administrative data elements for analytics more than others? This trend points toward limitations in the enabling conditions for government analytics. Data elements may not be readily accessible owing to limited data sharing among government organizations and weak interoperability among information systems. Even if data elements are accessible, infrastructure limitations may constrain their use. For example, human resources data on employees' attitudes and motivations usually come from surveys of public servants, which are often not integrated into HRMISs more broadly. Similarly, complaints data are often not integrated into standard e-Procurement systems and instead require integration with a separate complaints database. These challenges are described further in the discussion of data infrastructure later in the chapter.

How Do Governments Apply Analytics?

Government organizations in Latin America and the Caribbean mainly use analytical products based on administrative data for monitoring and accountability and to increase government transparency to citizens. More than 93 percent of respondents to the survey identified monitoring as the main application of analytics, 81 percent identified citizen transparency, and 79 percent mentioned accountability (figure 4.4). These findings align with the widespread adoption of control dashboards and open data initiatives across the region.

FIGURE 4.4 Applications of Analytical Products

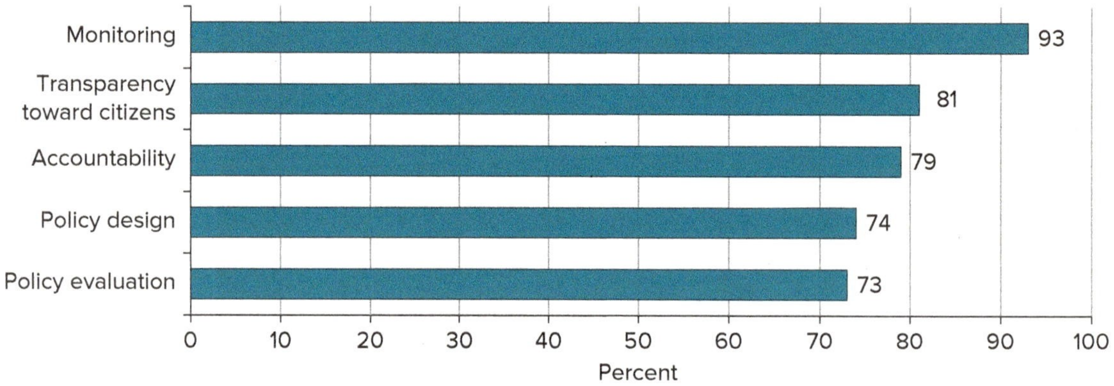

Application	Percent
Monitoring	93
Transparency toward citizens	81
Accountability	79
Policy design	74
Policy evaluation	73

Source: Government Analytics Survey in Latin America and the Caribbean.
Note: The figure shows the proportion of MISs in the region that are used for each application. The results do not total 100 percent because the question allowed for multiple responses. $N = 85$ country-MISs. MISs = management information systems.

Governments in the region use administrative data analytics less frequently for policy evaluation and design; however, for some government functions, this difference is not substantial (figure 4.5). The widespread use of analytics for monitoring and accountability represents a commendable first step toward a more accountable public administration. Likewise, the more limited use of analytics for policy evaluation and design represents an opportunity to use administrative data more strategically to improve government functioning by expanding the scope of these applications of analytics.

How Is Government Analytics Distributed?

As noted in the conceptual framework in chapter 2, analytics production can be ad hoc, bureaucratic, or strategic. Most respondents to the survey described analytics production in their organizations as strategic, meaning that their organizations produce analytics continuously in response to an overall strategic plan. The resulting analytical products often take the form of data dashboards for control purposes. However, not all MIS analytics production follows this pattern. HRMIS analytics production is primarily bureaucratic, reflecting a focus on regulatory compliance rather than strategic insights (figure 4.6).

FIGURE 4.5 Applications of Analytical Products, by Type of MIS

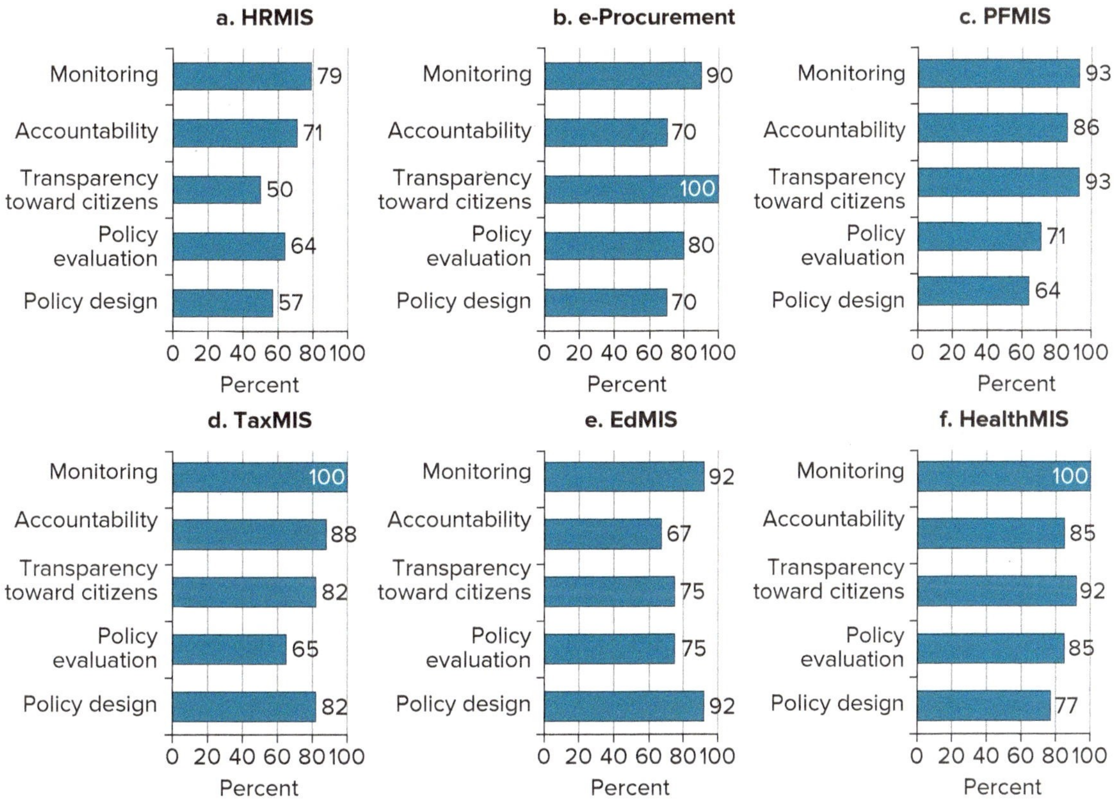
a. HRMIS
Monitoring
79
Accountability
71
Transparency toward citizens
50
Policy evaluation
64
Policy design
57
0 20 40 60 80 100
Percent
b. e-Procurement
Monitoring
90
Accountability
70
Transparency toward citizens
100
Policy evaluation
80
Policy design
70
0 20 40 60 80 100
Percent
c. PFMIS
Monitoring
93
Accountability
86
Transparency toward citizens
93
Policy evaluation
71
Policy design
64
0 20 40 60 80 100
Percent
d. TaxMIS
Monitoring
100
Accountability
88
Transparency toward citizens
82
Policy evaluation
65
Policy design
82
0 20 40 60 80 100
Percent
e. EdMIS
Monitoring
92
Accountability
67
Transparency toward citizens
75
Policy evaluation
75
Policy design
92
0 20 40 60 80 100
Percent
f. HealthMIS
Monitoring
100
Accountability
85
Transparency toward citizens
92
Policy evaluation
85
Policy design
77
0 20 40 60 80 100
Percent

Source: Government Analytics Survey in Latin America and the Caribbean.
Note: The figure shows, by type of MIS, the proportion of systems in the region that are used for each application. The results for each type of MIS do not total 100 percent because the question allowed for multiple responses. N = 85 country-MISs, distributed as follows: EdMIS questionnaire (n = 13 countries); e-Procurement questionnaire (n = 11 countries); HealthMIS questionnaire (n = 14 countries); HRMIS questionnaire (n = 14 countries); PFMIS questionnaire (n = 16 countries); TaxMIS questionnaire (n = 17 countries). EdMIS = education management information system; e-Procurement = procurement management information system; HealthMIS = health management information system; HRMIS = human resources management information system; MIS = management information system; PFMIS = public financial management information system; TaxMIS = tax management information system.

FIGURE 4.6 Kinds of Analytical Production, by Type of MIS

```
Percent
         HRMIS        e-Procurement    PFMIS         TaxMIS        EdMIS        HealthMIS
Ad hoc:    23              11            15            20            0             31
Bureaucratic: 46           33            31             7           25              8
Strategic: 31              56            54            73           75             62
```

Source: Government Analytics Survey in Latin America and the Caribbean.
Note: The figure shows, by type of MIS, the proportion of systems in the region that produce analytical products in an ad hoc, bureaucratic, or strategic manner. N = 85 country-MISs, distributed as follows: EdMIS questionnaire (*n* = 13 countries); e-Procurement questionnaire (*n* = 11 countries); HealthMIS questionnaire (*n* = 14 countries); HRMIS questionnaire (*n* = 14 countries); PFMIS questionnaire (*n* = 16 countries); TaxMIS questionnaire (*n* = 17 countries). EdMIS = education management information system; e-Procurement = procurement management information system; HealthMIS = health management information system; HRMIS = human resources management information system; MIS = management information system; PFMIS = public financial management information system; TaxMIS = tax management information system.

WHAT ANALYTICAL CAPABILITIES DO GOVERNMENTS IN THE REGION POSSESS?

As described in the conceptual framework in chapter 2, analytical capabilities—including adequate staffing, career and skill development, and funding opportunities—are an essential enabling condition for government analytics. The results of the survey suggest that governments in Latin America and the Caribbean have significant room to develop their analytical capabilities.

Governments in the region face a shortage of structured career development opportunities in analytics, which are essential for attracting and retaining skilled data analysts in the public sector. Only 12 percent of governments have a dedicated career track for data analysts (figure 4.7). For this reason, many digital MIS projects in the region suffer a progressive loss of human resources to other projects that offer better career prospects or higher salaries (Porrúa et al. 2021). When governments lack career incentives for data analysts, they can significantly undermine the investments they have made in recruiting and training these skilled personnel (OECD 2014).

FIGURE 4.7 Career Tracks for and Training and Assessments on Analytics

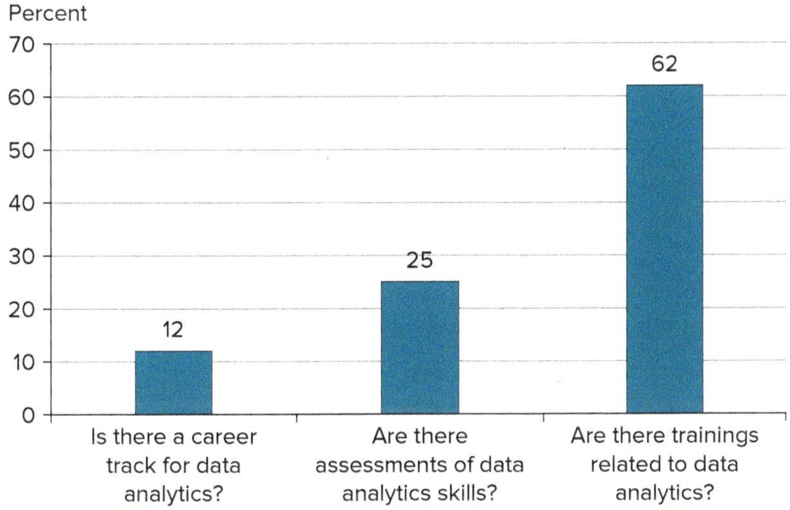

Source: Government Analytics Survey in Latin America and the Caribbean.
Note: The figure shows the proportion of surveyed countries in Latin America and the Caribbean for which the answer to each question is yes. *n* = 16 countries.

Governments in Latin America and the Caribbean also offer few options for capacity assessment and data analytics training (figure 4.7), and the options that do exist are not closely integrated with a strategic plan or work program on government analytics. Of the countries surveyed, 62 percent report that they offer training programs to strengthen the analytical capabilities of the public sector workforce. The range of these training options is wide, encompassing different formats, durations, content, and objectives. However, only 25 percent of the countries surveyed assess their staffs' proficiency in data analytics. In addition, existing training programs were described by the digital government experts surveyed as sporadic and sometimes as lacking a cohesive structure and a clear pathway for applying newly acquired skills in existing work programs. To be effective, capacity-building programs should be designed based on an assessment of the analytical skills that already exist in the public sector workforce in relation to medium- and long-term needs for analytical expertise. Governments that do not assess the skills public servants have and compare them with strategic goals risk offering training that does not reflect the skills public servants need.

> "Data analyst positions exist throughout the administration, but there is no specifically designed career progression for these roles."
> – Digital government expert

As these findings underscore, governments in the region need more structured efforts to cultivate analytical expertise within government organizations, as well as a more strategic approach to establish analytics production as a core work stream in public administration. Organizations need stable, dedicated funding to produce analytical products, establish workflows that closely connect policy needs to analytics production, and build analytical capabilities within government organizations. However, many organizations face significant challenges in securing consistent funding for analytical initiatives, because resources are limited and priorities often shift rapidly. Funding for analytics must be balanced against competing needs in the general government budget.

To mitigate these challenges, organizations should secure funding for analytics through careful consideration, strategic planning, and a long-term vision. Only 33 percent of surveyed experts reported that their governments offer internal funding opportunities for analytical initiatives. As figure 4.8 illustrates, internal funding opportunities appear more widespread for analytical projects related to education and health (46 and 43 percent of MISs, respectively).

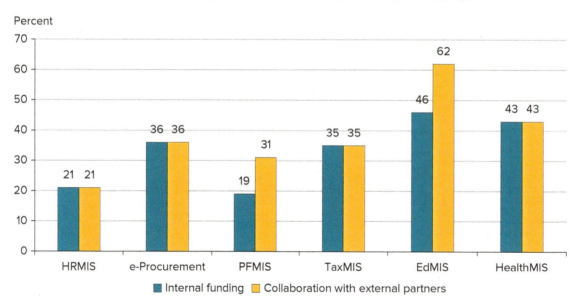

FIGURE 4.8 Opportunities for Internal Funding and Collaboration with Academics, Nonprofits, or Multilateral Organizations on Analytics Projects, by Type of MIS

Source: Government Analytics Survey in Latin America and the Caribbean.
Note: The figure shows, by type of MIS, the proportion of systems in the region that have internal funding opportunities available for developing analytical products or that have collaborations with external partners on data analytics. N = 85 country-MISs, distributed as follows: EdMIS questionnaire (n = 13 countries); e-Procurement questionnaire (n = 11 countries); HealthMIS questionnaire (n = 14 countries); HRMIS questionnaire (n = 14 countries); PFMIS questionnaire (n = 16 countries); TaxMIS questionnaire (n = 17 countries). EdMIS = education management information system; e-Procurement = procurement management information system; HealthMIS = health management information system; HRMIS = human resources management information system; MIS = management information system; PFMIS = public financial management information system; TaxMIS = tax management information system.

> "Public budgets are limited, so funding gaps are identified to request alignment and support through international cooperation."
>
> – PFMIS expert

Support from international organizations and donors can help fill these gaps. The primary driver of collaboration on data analytics with external partners is a need for technical assistance (figure 4.9), suggesting a strategic opportunity for government organizations to leverage external expertise to enhance analytics, particularly where internal resources and capabilities are limited. However, the same government functions that are more likely to receive internal funding are also more likely to collaborate strategically on analytical projects with academics, nonprofits, or multilateral organizations. Internal funding opportunities and external collaborations for analytical projects based on HRMIS, e-Procurement, PFMIS, or TaxMIS data appear to be very limited (less than 36 percent of respondents reported them), as shown in figure 4.8.

FIGURE 4.9 Drivers of Collaboration on Analytics with Academics, Nonprofits, or Multilateral Organizations

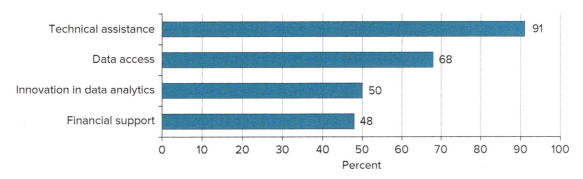

Source: Government Analytics Survey in Latin America and the Caribbean.
Note: The figure shows the proportion of MISs in the region for which each described category is a driver of collaboration on data analytics with external partners. The results do not total 100 percent because the question allowed for multiple responses. *N* = 85 country-MISs. MIS = management information system.

> "We collaborate on request, but not as part of a strategy."
>
> – TaxMIS expert

> "The institutional budget does not include a specific item for research or data analysis; however, it does include the payment of salaries for the institutional staff, which means that there is indirect budgetary support."
> – PFMIS expert

Governments in the region can also systematize the use of analytics in decision-making by incorporating dedicated analytics units into the organizational structure of public administration. Analytics units can help the government attract data analysts; establish a consistent, long-term analytical work stream; and secure regular funding through the payroll of dedicated staff. Nearly 80 percent of the experts surveyed reported that their governments have specialized units tasked with producing analytics using administrative data. However, many respondents noted that these units are not exclusively dedicated to analytics, as they split their working time between analytical tasks and operational functions as needed. Only a few respondents mentioned an innovation lab or a dedicated analytics team that focuses full-time on producing analytics. Relying on part-time teams for analytical tasks can lead to suboptimal outcomes because these teams might assign immediate operational needs a higher priority than broader analytical objectives, missing opportunities for innovation, optimization, and long-term planning for evidence-based policy making.

WHAT IS THE STATE OF DATA INFRASTRUCTURE IN THE REGION?

As described in the conceptual framework in chapter 2, data infrastructure is also a key enabling condition for government analytics. Outdated or inadequate data infrastructure limits data quality and accessibility, making it difficult for organizations to use administrative data for analytics and policy making. Data infrastructure problems hinder the development of analytics in
Latin America and the Caribbean: although the region is a global pioneer in establishing MISs (as discussed in chapter 1), 61 percent of the MIS experts surveyed reported that their MISs are not fully digitalized.

Levels of MIS digitalization vary substantially by government function (figure 4.10). TaxMISs and PFMISs exhibit a relatively high degree of digitalization (71 and 50 percent of these types of MIS, respectively, are fully digitalized), whereas HealthMISs have the lowest degree of digitalization. In the health sector, only 8 percent of respondents reported that their HealthMIS is fully digitalized. According to MIS experts, some information is still recorded in Word documents, PDFs, and Excel spreadsheets. Levels of digitalization also vary significantly across different types of MIS within a single country (figure 4.11). Although some countries have more fully digitalized MISs than others, TaxMISs are consistently the most advanced.

FIGURE 4.10 Fully Digitalized Systems, by Type of MIS

Type	Percent
TaxMIS	71
PFMIS	50
EdMIS	46
e-Procurement	30
HRMIS	21
HealthMIS	8

Source: Government Analytics Survey in Latin America and the Caribbean.
Note: The figure shows, by type of MIS, the proportion of systems in the region that are fully digitalized. N = 85 country-MISs, distributed as follows: EdMIS questionnaire (n = 13 countries); e-Procurement questionnaire (n = 11 countries); HealthMIS questionnaire (n = 14 countries); HRMIS questionnaire (n = 14 countries); PFMIS questionnaire (n = 16 countries); TaxMIS questionnaire (n = 17 countries). EdMIS = education management information system; e-Procurement = procurement management information system; HealthMIS = health management information system; HRMIS = human resources management information system; MIS = management information system; PFMIS = public financial management information system; TaxMIS = tax management information system.

FIGURE 4.11 Fully Digitalized Systems, by Country and Type of MIS

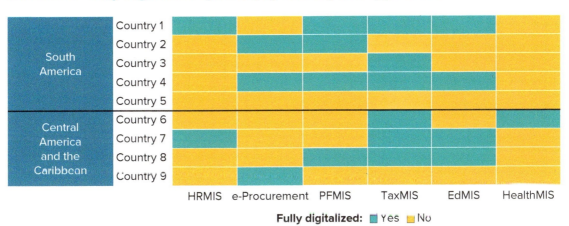

Source: Government Analytics Survey in Latin America and the Caribbean.
Note: The figure shows the level of system digitalization across MISs and countries in the region. The data presented include only countries that completed all six MIS questionnaires. n = 54 country-MISs. EdMIS = education management information system; e-Procurement = procurement management information system; HealthMIS = health management information system; HRMIS = human resources management information system; MIS = management information system; PFMIS = public financial management information system; TaxMIS = tax management information system.

> "e-Procurement is partially digitalized: Word documents, PDFs, images, Excel, and CSV [comma-separated values] files are still used."
>
> – e-Procurement expert

Why is digitalization limited to some government functions? MIS experts surveyed indicated that data fragmentation and isolated systems constrain digitalization: for example, when health records are kept in physical form, steps in the procurement cycle happen outside the government's e-Procurement system, or payroll information and data on performance evaluations and career trajectories are kept in separate systems. Fragmentation might also occur if different ministries use different procurement systems, or if different hospitals have different portals to record information on services provided. When systems are fragmented, various subsystems operate independently, and some are digitalized but others are not. This makes it virtually impossible to create a centralized, fully digitalized MIS with detailed, accurate, and updated information, preventing governments from effectively leveraging administrative data.

Fragmentation also means government organizations are unable to access and use each other's administrative data, preventing them from combining data from multiple sources to generate new evidence. Data sharing between government organizations is constrained by the inadequacy of formal access protocols for administrative data. These protocols serve two purposes: they help uphold trust in the agency responsible for producing the data, and they ensure uninterrupted access to the data over time.

> "The Ministry of Public Health has 103 information systems, most of which are not interoperable."
>
> – HealthMIS expert

> "The MIS is composed of various modules for managing the human talent subsystems; however, some of these modules to date are still not fully automated or digitalized."
>
> – HRMIS expert

> "There is no single protocol; each collaboration derives from an agreement that regulates the rules of relationship, and we have policies and standards for the use and handling of data."
> — HealthMIS expert
>
> "There is a verbal system in place [for data access], but no formal written procedure."
> — HealthMIS expert

Although they do exist—57 percent of MIS experts reported that there are formal protocols governing access to administrative data—many of these protocols appear to be ad hoc arrangements between the organization that manages an MIS and those seeking data access. These ad hoc agreements often lack explicit and standardized guidelines and requirements for and restrictions on data sharing.

According to some MIS experts, data accessibility is facilitated by laws governing open data initiatives. These laws, however, are typically designed with external consumers in mind, not internal government actors. Consequently, data provided through these initiatives may not be at a level of granularity sufficient to generate valuable insights about the functioning of public administration. In contrast, according to the Organisation for Economic Co-operation and Development's Digital Government Index, 96 percent of the organization's member countries outside Latin America and the Caribbean report having an explicit formal requirement for data sharing between government organizations (OECD 2019).[2] Without more formal protocols in Latin America and the Caribbean, data may be accessible only to those agencies that have the political leverage to negotiate for access.

However, just as is the case with analytical applications and capabilities, formal access protocols vary across different government functions. As figure 4.12 illustrates, access protocols seem to be more prevalent for HRMISs (86 percent), e-Procurement systems (73 percent), and TaxMISs (71 percent), whereas they are less common for EdMISs and HealthMISs (38 percent and 14 percent, respectively). This pattern also holds within countries: even if most MISs in a country have formal protocols for managing and sharing data, HealthMISs and EdMISs are exceptions (figure 4.13). This variation may be due to different regulatory frameworks, levels of data fragmentation, organizational priorities, or levels of stakeholder engagement across the agencies managing these information systems. For HealthMISs, the absence of formal access protocols may also be caused by their low degree of digitalization, as noted earlier.

FIGURE 4.12 Formal Data Access Protocols, by Type of MIS

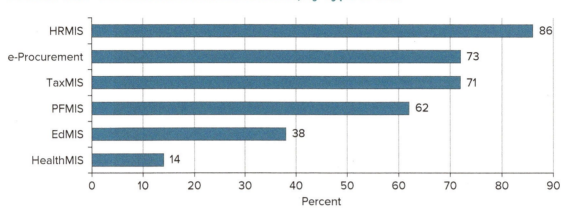

Source: Government Analytics Survey in Latin America and the Caribbean.
Note: The figure shows, by type of MIS, the proportion of systems in the region that have formal protocols for accessing system data. N = 85 country-MISs, distributed as follows: EdMIS questionnaire (*n* = 13 countries); e-Procurement questionnaire (*n* = 11 countries); HealthMIS questionnaire (*n* = 14 countries); HRMIS questionnaire (*n* = 14 countries); PFMIS questionnaire (*n* = 16 countries); TaxMIS questionnaire (*n* = 17 countries). EdMIS = education management information system; e-Procurement = procurement management information system; HealthMIS = health management information system; HRMIS = human resources management information system; MIS = management information system; PFMIS = public financial management information system; TaxMIS = tax management information system.

FIGURE 4.13 Formal Data Access Protocols, by Country and Type of MIS

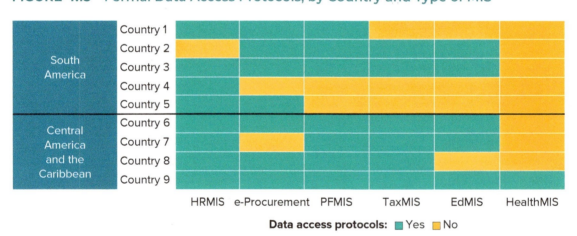

Source: Government Analytics Survey in Latin America and the Caribbean.
Note: The figure shows the existence of formal protocols for accessing system data across MISs and countries in the region. The data presented include only countries that completed all six MIS questionnaires. *n* = 54 country-MISs. EdMIS = education management information system; e-Procurement = procurement management information system; HealthMIS = health management information system; HRMIS = human resources management information system; MIS = management information system; PFMIS = public financial management information system; TaxMIS = tax management information system.

> "The HealthMIS is only partially digitalized due to the existence of some physical forms that are not integrated into the system."
>
> – HealthMIS expert

Data accessibility is also limited when organizations lack systematized information on the data available in information systems. According to more than half (58 percent) of MIS experts surveyed, comprehensive data inventories, which list all available data elements within an MIS, do not exist for the systems they work with. Without data inventories, organizations struggle to determine what types of data are available and where they are stored, which makes it more complicated for them to conceive and implement new analytical projects. Additionally, without comprehensive documentation, organizations cannot properly manage data throughout their life cycles, from creation and storage to archiving or deletion. Furthermore, only 15 percent of MISs measure how often their data are accessed. More robust and standardized approaches to tracking administrative data access are important to identify users and frequency of use and optimize data utilization by organizations.

In addition to being comprehensive and accessible, data must also be high in quality, so MISs need mechanisms to ensure the quality of the data they contain. According to the majority (65 percent) of MIS experts surveyed, data quality controls are implemented in the systems they work with to ensure the accuracy, consistency, completeness, reliability, and overall quality of administrative data. These controls seem to be particularly prevalent for TaxMISs (82 percent) and EdMISs (85 percent), but they are less frequent for HealthMISs (43 percent) (figure 4.14). However, these

> "Inventories exist, but they do not frame or contain all the data."
>
> – HealthMIS expert
>
> "There is no organized record of the available data."
>
> – PFMIS expert
>
> "There are usage metrics for the platform in general, but not specifically regarding data access."
>
> – TaxMIS expert

MIS experts also noted that data-cleaning processes are often infrequent and must be performed manually, outside the systems. Indeed, according to the World Bank's GovTech Maturity Index, only 25 percent of countries in the region have implemented a data quality framework, which is lower than the implementation rate in other regions (World Bank 2022).[3]

FIGURE 4.14 Data Quality Controls in Place, by Type of MIS

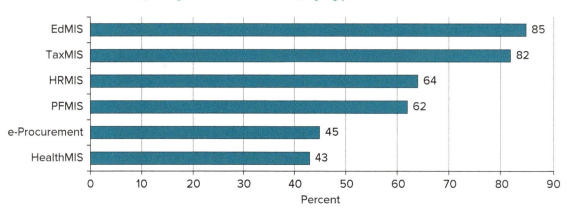

Source: Government Analytics Survey in Latin America and the Caribbean.
Note: The figure shows, by type of MIS, the proportion of systems in the region that have data quality controls in place. N = 85 country-MISs, distributed as follows: EdMIS questionnaire (n = 13 countries); e-Procurement questionnaire (n = 11 countries); HealthMIS questionnaire (n = 14 countries); HRMIS questionnaire (n = 14 countries); PFMIS questionnaire (n = 16 countries); TaxMIS questionnaire (n = 17 countries). EdMIS = education management information system; e-Procurement = procurement management information system; HealthMIS = health management information system; HRMIS = human resources management information system; MIS = management information system; PFMIS = public financial management information system; TaxMIS = tax management information system.

This lack of systematic data quality controls can pose problems for organizations seeking to leverage administrative data for analytics. When data quality controls are not integrated into an MIS, each team accessing the data needs to perform its own quality controls, duplicating other teams' efforts. This results in a highly inefficient quality control process. Moreover, if quality issues, such as erroneous data input or incomplete data fields, remain, they can significantly undermine the accuracy, reliability, and replicability of analytics.

> "There are some quality control checks and auditing processes in place; however, additional controls are necessary moving forward to ensure the optimum quality of data."
>
> — **HealthMIS expert**

> "Although there are no data-cleaning processes, work is being done to improve the data and their quality by means of validation upon entry and correction requests."
> — TaxMIS expert
>
> "There are quality controls in the transactional system that provides data for e-Procurement, but they are not sufficient for adequate data quality."
> — e-Procurement expert
>
> "Data are reviewed on a regular basis, but it is labor-intensive with the lack of appropriate tools; hence, more can be done."
> — HRMIS expert

All the data infrastructure limitations mentioned here—incomplete digitalization; data fragmentation; and the lack of formal access protocols, comprehensive data inventories, and systematic data quality controls—weaken the interoperability of government information systems. If governments established the foundational infrastructure for interoperability, they could thus advance their overall potential for using data for analytics and policy making enormously. According to the World Bank's GovTech Maturity Index, less than 35 percent of countries in Latin America and the Caribbean have implemented a government interoperability framework that allows efficient and secure information exchange between government systems and organizations (World Bank 2022).[4] Governments should transition from a fragmented, siloed approach to a comprehensive, whole-of-government approach to ensure responsive, effective public administration. This means that rather than requiring individual organizations to collect, store, and analyze data in isolation to pursue organization-specific objectives, governments should encourage collaboration among organizations spanning different levels and sectors. Such a collaborative approach can foster synergy and help organizations achieve shared objectives across diverse domains.

Overall, the regional assessment presented in this chapter reveals the enormous potential for governments in Latin America and the Caribbean to use their existing administrative data to enhance policy design and implementation. By enhancing their analytical capabilities (through building dedicated analytical career tracks and dedicated analytics units) and by strengthening their data infrastructure (through enhancing data quality controls and strengthening MIS interoperability), governments can build on their existing use of descriptive analytics for monitoring and accountability. Diagnostic and predictive analytics, if developed strategically and in response to policy needs, can help advance evidence-based policy making and strengthen government functioning in the region. The final chapter of this report lays out policy recommendations to show how governments can strengthen their overall government analytics ecosystem to pursue these goals.

NOTES

1. All analyses in this chapter are presented at aggregate levels. Individual countries are not identified owing to data confidentiality agreements for the survey. Keeping countries anonymous and informing respondents of this approach beforehand likely reduced social desirability bias in their responses.
2. The 2019 Digital Government Index question reads as follows: "Does your country have an explicit formal requirement for public sector organizations to share the data they produce with other public sector organizations?"
3. Only Africa (excluding North Africa) has a lower implementation rate than Latin America and the Caribbean, with just 13 percent of countries having implemented a data quality framework. In comparison, 51 percent of countries in Europe and Central Asia, 50 percent of countries in South Asia, 33 percent of countries in the Middle East and North Africa, and 30 percent of countries in East Asia and the Pacific have implemented data quality frameworks (World Bank 2022).
4. The implementation rate for data interoperability frameworks in Latin America and the Caribbean is significantly lower than those in South Asia (75 percent) and Europe and Central Asia (74 percent), but it is higher than those in the Middle East and North Africa (33 percent), East Asia and Pacific (27 percent), and Africa (23 percent) (World Bank 2022).

REFERENCES

OECD (Organisation for Economic Co-operation and Development). 2014. "Recommendation of the Council on Digital Government Strategies." Adopted July 14, 2014. https://legalinstruments.oecd.org/en/instruments/OECD-LEGAL-0406.

OECD (Organisation for Economic Co-operation and Development). 2019. "Digital Government Index: 2019 Results." OECD Public Governance Policy Paper 3, OECD, Paris. https://doi.org/10.1787/4de9f5bb-en.

Porrúa, Miguel, Mariano Lafuente, Benjamin Roseth, Laura Ripani, Edgardo Mosqueira, Angela Reyes, Javier Fuenzalida, Francisco Suárez, and Rodrigo Salas. 2021. *Digital Transformation and Public Employment: The Future of Government Work*. Washington, DC: Inter-American Development Bank. https://doi.org/10.18235/0003245.

World Bank. 2022. *GovTech Maturity Index, 2022 Update: Trends in Public Sector Digital Transformation*. Equitable Growth, Finance and Institutions Insight—Governance. Washington, DC: World Bank. https://hdl.handle.net/10986/38499.

CHAPTER 5

Policy Recommendations to Strengthen Government Analytics in Latin America and the Caribbean

INTRODUCTION

This report has offered an overview and analysis of how governments in Latin America and the Caribbean can use data analytics to address development challenges. It has argued that governments in the region can take advantage of significant advances in management information system (MIS) coverage to develop analytics strategically and apply them to policy design, implementation, and evaluation, especially by strengthening the enabling conditions for these advances: analytical capabilities and data infrastructure. The report's conceptual framework (chapter 2), case studies (chapter 3), and regional assessment (chapter 4) offer governments guidance in developing a government analytics ecosystem in their context and inspiration for the many ways analytics can be applied to drive evidence-based policy making and improve government functioning.

This chapter offers targeted policy recommendations to help governments put the other chapters of this report into practice by developing and using data analytics to further their own policy objectives. The policy recommendations reflect the structure of the conceptual framework (figure 2.1). First, the chapter discusses how to move toward a more strategic approach to government analytics to generate evidence for decision-making. Then, it presents recommendations for building analytical capabilities, and finally, it looks at ways to strengthen data infrastructure.

A reproducibility package is available for this book in the Reproducible Research Repository at https://reproducibility.worldbank.org/index.php/catalog/209.

These policy recommendations can be used by government organizations that are just beginning to leverage their administrative data as well as those that are already far along their analytics journey. As the regional assessment in chapter 4 shows, MIS digitalization, data access protocols, and quality controls can vary widely across government functions within a single country. For this reason, this chapter breaks most of the recommendations down into strategic steps of increasing complexity. Organizations can approach these steps in order, and they can use them to identify the appropriate next step in their own contexts.

Identifying next steps is important because developing a strong government analytics ecosystem is an iterative process. When governments push data collection and analytics to the limit, they can put pressure on public servants, resulting in perverse incentives that limit the power of analytics to inform decision-making. Under pressure, organizations might have incentives to focus only on measuring what is easiest to quantify, resulting in a partial or distorted understanding of phenomena and taking attention away from analyzing their foundational causes. Public servants might even face pressure to falsify or misrepresent data, threatening the health of the analytics ecosystem as a whole (Bridges and Woolcock 2023).

One way that governments can avoid creating these distortionary incentives is by approaching analytics strategically and incrementally, while paying attention to how analytical initiatives depend on and transform enabling conditions within the analytics ecosystem. By focusing on targeted, gradual reforms, governments do not sacrifice the significant impact of analytics, because even slightly better analytics can lead to large improvements in government functioning. As the case studies in this report have shown, government organizations that take small, initial steps toward analytics—like organizing a datathon or developing descriptive analytics about health appointments—can still make a large impact.

POLICY RECOMMENDATIONS

How Can Governments Move toward a More Strategic Approach to Analytics to Generate Evidence for Decision-Making?

As outlined in chapter 4, administrative data in Latin America and the Caribbean are predominantly used for descriptive analytics. Diagnostic and predictive analytics remain largely underutilized, hindering governments' ability to effectively anticipate and respond to policy challenges. Furthermore, analytical products are primarily employed for monitoring and accountability, with less emphasis on policy evaluation and design. Relying on administrative data for operational and transactional purposes often results in missed opportunities to leverage advanced analytics for more strategic decision-making. These findings underscore the need for a more strategic approach to government analytics, which is reflected in the following recommendations.

Strengthen the culture for evidence-based policy making and the demand for analytics within public administration.

1. Review whether data and evidence are being used to define policies and strategies in each government function. (For detailed information on analytical initiatives and decision-making in human resources, public finance, and procurement, refer to chapters 10–12 of *The Government Analytics Handbook* [Tavares, Ortega Nieto, and Woodhouse 2023; Piatti-Fünfkirchen, Brumby, and Hashim 2023; Cocciolo, Samaddar, and Fazekas 2023].)

2. Strengthen the link between analytics applications and decision-making by systematically defining the priorities for reform in each government function and the evidence that would be needed to guide reform in that function. (For example: What could be improved about procurement? What would governments need to know to make those improvements?)

3. Build demand for data analytics through workshops, conferences, and programs that create awareness of effective applications of analytics, establish networks and partnerships, and encourage data sharing among government organizations. (For more information on data sharing, refer, for example, to Welch, Feeney, and Park 2016.)

4. Strengthen partnerships among organizations and coordinate public stakeholders' interests (refer, for example, to Allard et al. 2018).

5. Once demand for data analytics has been established, design and implement an institutional data governance strategy and a data management strategy. These strategic documents are essential to enable government organizations to effectively manage their data assets; create internal protocols, processes, roles, and policies; mitigate risks; and strengthen a culture that supports evidence-based decision-making. (For more details on data governance, refer to chapters 6 and 8 of the *World Development Report 2021: Data for Better Lives* [World Bank 2021].)

Define the strategic use of government data.

1. Review how data from each MIS could be used to inform decision-making in the related government function. (For example: How can e-Procurement data be used to strengthen procurement?)

2. Strategize about the broader uses of data from each MIS *across* organizations, especially if they are connected with other government data. (For example: What can e-Procurement data be used for besides procurement? Which organizations are currently using procurement data and how? Which organizations would benefit from using procurement data and how?)

Streamline descriptive analytics and develop diagnostic and predictive analytics.

1. Create the conditions for effective and efficient use of administrative data for monitoring and accountability. Define a monitoring and accountability framework, establish a process for creating regular reports based on administrative data, and create an interactive dashboard for control and reporting purposes.

2. Move toward using diagnostic and predictive analytics to inform policy evaluation and design. Develop more advanced analytical products, such as (for procurement) red-flag systems, bid-rigging screening tools, or government risk assessment systems (case study 3.11). Progressing from descriptive to diagnostic and predictive analytics can unleash great potential from government data, but it requires political support to shift how policy decisions are made as well as strong foundations in data infrastructure and analytical capabilities. Predictive analytics also requires data analysts with more advanced technical skills, partnerships with external institutions, or both.

How Can Governments Build Analytical Capabilities for Individuals and Organizations?

The report identifies a critical need to strengthen analytical capabilities in both individuals and organizations within the public sector of Latin America and the Caribbean. Although governments in the region recognize the importance of analytical skills, there is a significant gap in structured career tracks for data analysts and a lack of systematic proficiency evaluations in data analytics for public servants. This deficiency, coupled with limited funding for analytical projects, constrains the development and implementation of comprehensive analytics strategies. The findings suggest that establishing dedicated analytics units and fostering collaborations with academic and international organizations can play a pivotal role in addressing these capacity-building challenges. These strategies are essential for enhancing the strategic use of data analytics in government decision-making.

Assess existing analytical capabilities.

1. Assess analytical capabilities in the public sector regularly, especially in dedicated analytics units (if they exist). Use these assessments to identify capacity-building needs and shape strategic workforce planning.

2. Align the analytical capabilities of the public sector workforce with the skills and expertise needed for the strategic production and use of government analytics.

Build analytical capabilities strategically.

1. Offer training programs in data analytics and develop initiatives to strengthen public servants' capacity to use data and evidence to make key decisions.

2. Develop a coherent framework for connecting skills development to practical applications, integrating training and capacity building into an overall strategy to move public administration toward evidence-based policy making. Approaching data analytics training programs strategically can help ensure that they have a cohesive structure and offer clear pathways for trainees to apply newly acquired skills within existing work programs.

3. For decision-makers, build capacity to identify knowledge gaps and evidence needs and apply analytical insights.

4. For data analysts, complement training programs with sector-specific technical training when necessary. It is essential that analytics teams understand the context and implications of analytics in specific policy areas.

5. For subject area experts, build capacity to identify knowledge gaps, design analytical initiatives, interpret analytical results, and put results into context.

Establish a dedicated career track for analysts.

1. Establish a dedicated career track for data analysts in the public sector to generate structured career development opportunities in analytics, which are essential for attracting and retaining skilled data analysts.

2. Build relationships with academic institutions to create opportunities for attracting and fostering specialized talent through internships, fellowships, and educational leave with pay for public officials. (For more information, refer to chapter 6 of Porrúa et al. 2021.)

Establish dedicated analytics units.

1. Establish a unit within the organizational structure of public administration whose mandate is to use government data for monitoring, evaluation, reporting, policy design, and research. Consider whether a centralized unit, which provides analytics for the entire administration, or decentralized units, which focus on specific government functions within a single organization, are better in the given context.

2. Leverage analytics units to attract data analysts; establish a consistent, long-term analytical work stream; and secure regular funding through the payroll of dedicated staff.

Secure a budget to support analytical capabilities and products.

A dedicated budget is essential for supporting analytical products (such as dashboards, reports, and research) and capacity building.

1. Offer internal funding opportunities for analytical initiatives.

2. Leverage analytics units and external collaborations to secure resources for data analytics and mitigate budget constraints.

3. Share funding for analytics teams with other public institutions through formal or informal arrangements to reduce costs and promote data interoperability and knowledge exchange.

4. Develop a strategic plan and a long-term vision to make data analytics a priority within the government budget.

Develop external collaborations to support all the recommendations in this chapter.

1. Develop strategies to collaborate on analytics and research with academics, nonprofits, foundations, or multilateral organizations. External partners can help mitigate budget constraints. They can also address a lack of analytical skills and expertise in public administration by helping to design and implement analytical products. Collaborations require a clear framework for data sharing and the coproduction of analytical products.

2. Consider partnerships with the educational sector to build capabilities. Globally, universities are launching initiatives to address a lack of analytical skills in the labor market. Governments, as major employers, can play a crucial role in these efforts. For instance, Uruguay has forged a productive partnership with the Universidad de la República, resulting in the creation of an ongoing education course, "Data Quality Management for Digital Government." This course is specifically designed to help public servants working on public sector digital transformation develop specialized analytical skills.

How Can Governments Strengthen Data Infrastructure?

The report highlights significant challenges in the data infrastructure of Latin America and the Caribbean, despite advances in digitalization. Many MISs are insufficiently comprehensive or irregularly updated, resulting in significant variations in data quality. There is a notable lack of systematic data quality control measures, and data cleaning is often manual and sporadic. This situation hampers the accuracy, reliability, promptness, and replicability of data analytics. Additionally, limited interoperability among MISs and the ad hoc nature of data sharing among government organizations prevent the full potential of digitalized MISs from being realized in analytical projects. These issues underscore the critical need for improved data governance and robust infrastructure to support effective government analytics in the region.

Assess the quality, completeness, and timeliness of government data and define steps for improvement.

Regularly assessing, reviewing, and updating MISs is essential to catalyze the value of their data.

1. Ensure that MISs are fully digitalized. This requires transitioning away from manually recording information in Word documents, PDFs, or Excel spreadsheets. Because of resource constraints, certain data elements may need to be given priority over others.

2. Determine whether administrative data are correct, complete, timely, and available for analytics, and identify any obstacles to data quality.

3. When an MIS is part of a data ecosystem with a joint policy objective (for instance, the public financial management information ecosystem, which, in practice, includes several institutions and MISs), examine data quality, completeness, and timeliness in relation to the overall data ecosystem. Assess the quality of all MISs in the ecosystem to avoid information silos and strengthen less effective MISs.

Establish regular, systematic, and automated data quality controls.

Data quality issues, such as erroneous data input or incomplete data fields, can significantly undermine the accuracy, reliability, and replicability of analytics.

1. Integrate data quality controls (such as data cleaning, coverage, and harmonization) into MISs to make quality control more efficient and reliable.

2. Establish dedicated teams responsible for overseeing data quality controls.

Establish a data inventory.

A data inventory helps users determine what types of data are available in an MIS, where they are stored, and the exact definition of data fields. This makes it much easier to develop and implement new analytical projects. A data inventory is also necessary for the proper management of data throughout their life cycle, from creation and storage to archiving or deletion.

Connect government data.

1. Establish protocols for data sharing between government agencies. Establishing explicit, formal protocols for sharing administrative data is a key step toward connecting and integrating government data and producing more advanced analytical products. (For information on institutions, laws, and regulations to enhance data accessibility, refer to World Bank 2022.)

2. Integrate MISs to unlock the full potential of fully digitalized systems for analytics. (For details on data integration and systems interoperability, refer to World Bank 2023.)

Plan for MIS maintenance and updates.

Establish protocols for MIS maintenance and updates to ensure that MISs continually leverage the newest technological advances.

CONCLUSION

The policy recommendations that conclude this report present strategic steps that governments in Latin America and the Caribbean can take to promote the development of a government analytics ecosystem. By strengthening their analytical capabilities and data infrastructure holistically, governments can unlock the full potential of their administrative data while remaining responsive to decision-makers' needs for evidence in different policy areas. Government analytics that supports the knowledge and experience of policy makers and managers can be a key tool for creating a culture of evidence-based policy making within public administration, with positive impacts on fiscal sustainability, public service delivery, and citizens' trust in public institutions.

Over the past few decades, governments in Latin America and the Caribbean have built a strong foundation for data analytics and have experimented with different analytical applications. By drawing on the conceptual framework, case studies, regional assessment, and policy recommendations in this report, governments can further advance their use of administrative data for analytics. Government analytics initiatives can provide policy makers with the evidence needed to make informed decisions, address governance and development challenges, and build a more efficient and effective public administration.

REFERENCES

Allard, Scott W., Emily R. Wiegand, Colleen Schlecht, A. Rupa Datta, Robert M. Goerge, and Elizabeth Weigensberg. 2018. "State Agencies' Use of Administrative Data for Improved Practice: Needs, Challenges, and Opportunities." *Public Administration Review* 78 (2): 240–50. https://doi.org/10.1111/puar.12883.

Bridges, Kate, and Michael Woolcock. 2023. "Measuring What Matters: Principles for a Balanced Data Suite That Prioritizes Problem Solving and Learning." In *The Government Analytics Handbook: Leveraging Data to Strengthen Public Administration*, edited by Daniel Rogger and Christian Schuster, chap. 4. Washington, DC: World Bank. https://doi.org/10.1596/978-1-4648-1957-5.

Cocciolo, Serena, Suxhmita Samaddar, and Mihaly Fazekas. 2023. "Government Analytics Using Procurement Data." In *The Government Analytics Handbook: Leveraging Data to Strengthen Public Administration*, edited by Daniel Rogger and Christian Schuster, chap. 12. Washington, DC: World Bank. https://doi.org/10.1596/978-1-4648-1957-5.

Piatti-Fünfkirchen, James Brumby, and Ali Hashim. 2023. "Government Analytics Using Expenditure Data." In *The Government Analytics Handbook: Leveraging Data to Strengthen Public Administration*, edited by Daniel Rogger and Christian Schuster, chap. 10. Washington, DC: World Bank. https://doi.org/10.1596/978-1-4648-1957-5.

Porrúa, Miguel, Mariano Lafuente, Benjamin Roseth, Laura Ripani, Edgardo Mosqueira, Angela Reyes, Javier Fuenzalida, Francisco Suárez, and Rodrigo Salas. 2021. *Digital Transformation and Public Employment: The Future of Government Work*. Washington, DC: Inter-American Development Bank. https://doi.org/10.18235/0003245.

Tavares, Rafael Alves de Albuquerque, Daniel Ortega Nieto, and Eleanor Florence Woodhouse. 2023. "Government Analytics Using Human Resources and Payroll Data." In *The Government Analytics Handbook: Leveraging Data to Strengthen Public Administration*, edited by Daniel Rogger and Christian Schuster, chap. 10. Washington, DC: World Bank. https://doi.org/10.1596/978-1-4648-1957-5_ch10.

Welch, Eric W., Mary K. Feeney, and Chul Hyun Park. 2016. "Determinants of Data Sharing in U.S. City Governments." *Government Information Quarterly* 33 (3): 393–403. https://doi.org/10.1016/j.giq.2016.07.002.

World Bank. 2021. *World Development Report 2021: Data for Better Lives*. Washington, DC: World Bank. https://www.worldbank.org/en/publication/wdr2021.

World Bank. 2022. *GovTech Maturity Index, 2022 Update: Trends in Public Sector Digital Transformation*. Equitable Growth, Finance and Institutions Insight—Governance. Washington, DC: World Bank. https://hdl.handle.net/10986/38499.

World Bank. 2023. *Interoperability: Towards a Data-Driven Public Sector*. Equitable Growth, Finance and Institutions Insight—Governance. Washington, DC: World Bank. https://doi.org/10.1596/38520.

APPENDIX A
Survey Methodology

The questionnaires used in the government analytics survey conducted for this report were designed following the conceptual framework outlined in chapter 2 and benefited from the input of different teams within the World Bank's Governance Global Practice, as well as feedback from government and international organization experts. Each questionnaire for a particular type of management information system (MIS) consisted of 20 questions and was uniformly structured, with identical questions but response options tailored to that type of MIS, including yes/no and multiple-choice formats. Respondents were also asked to elaborate on their responses, provide detailed explanations, share relevant documentation, and offer additional comments to support their answers. The capabilities questionnaire consisted of four questions.

The survey team administered the questionnaires online via the SurveyCTO platform, ensuring that only one response per MIS per country was recorded. The team's outreach strategy involved multiple stages. Initially, the team reached out to the digital government authority in each country to identify focal points. These digital authorities were invited via an email that introduced the survey and requested the appointment of a focal point for further communication. The team then invited these focal points to an information session about the survey. The focal points were then responsible for coordinating with relevant MIS experts within their governments to collect responses to the MIS-level questionnaires. To streamline the process, the team conducted a thorough review of MIS experts across all 32 countries in the region and shared the information with the focal points to help them coordinate data collection efforts.

Data collection took place from November 2023 to March 2024. Throughout this period, the team hosted multiple information sessions with representatives from 21 countries in the region. These sessions aimed to clarify the survey's objectives, offer detailed guidance on navigating and completing the survey, and address any questions or concerns raised by government officials. In total, 20 countries participated in the survey. The team received 85 responses to the MIS-level questionnaires, and 16 countries responded to the capabilities questionnaire. The 85 responses to the MIS-level questionnaires were distributed as follows: 13 countries responded to the education management information system (EdMIS) questionnaire, 11 countries to the e-Procurement questionnaire, 14 countries to the health management information system (HealthMIS) questionnaire, 14 countries to the human resources management information system (HRMIS) questionnaire, 16 countries to the public financial management information system (PFMIS) questionnaire, and 17 countries to the tax management information system (TaxMIS) questionnaire. A detailed breakdown of respondents by country and organization is provided in table A.1, and table A.2 lists the participating countries by questionnaire.

The team meticulously reviewed all responses to ensure data consistency, comprehensiveness, and comparability while identifying areas needing further evidence or documentation. During this process, the team followed up with each country for additional information, clarification, and examples to better contextualize its responses.

TABLE A.1 Countries and Organizations That Participated in the Survey

Country	Participating organizations, by questionnaire
Bahamas, The	**Capabilities:** Department of Information and Communication Technology
Barbados	**Capabilities:** Ministry of Industry, Innovation, Science and Technology **HRMIS:** Ministry of the Public Service **TaxMIS:** Barbados Revenue Authority
Belize	**Capabilities:** Ministry of Public Utilities, Energy, Logistics and E-Governance **EdMIS:** Ministry of Education, Culture, Science and Technology **HealthMIS:** Ministry of Health and Wellness **HRMIS:** Ministry of the Public Service, Constitutional and Political Reform and Religious Affairs **PFMIS:** Ministry of Finance **TaxMIS:** Belize Tax Service, Ministry of Finance
Bolivia	**Capabilities:** Agencia de Gobierno Electrónico y Tecnologías de Información y Comunicación **EdMIS:** Ministerio de Educación **e-Procurement:** Ministerio de Economía y Finanzas Públicas **HealthMIS:** Ministerio de Salud y Deportes **HRMIS:** Ministerio de Economía y Finanzas Públicas **PFMIS:** Ministerio de Economía y Finanzas Públicas **TaxMIS:** Servicio de Impuestos Nacionales
Brazil	**Capabilities:** Ministério da Gestão e da Inovação em Serviços Públicos **PFMIS:** Secretaria do Tesouro Nacional **TaxMIS:** Secretaria Especial da Receita Federal
Chile	**Capabilities:** Secretaría de Gobierno Digital **EdMIS:** Ministerio de Educación **e-Procurement:** ChileCompra **HealthMIS:** Ministerio de Salud **HRMIS:** Servicio Civil **PFMIS:** Ministerio de Hacienda **TaxMIS:** Servicio de Impuestos Internos
Colombia	**PFMIS:** Ministerio de Hacienda **TaxMIS:** Dirección de Impuestos y Aduanas Nacionales

(continues on next page)

TABLE A.1 Countries and Organizations That Participated in the Survey *(continued)*

Country	Participating organizations, by questionnaire
Costa Rica	**Capabilities:** Ministerio de Ciencia, Innovación, Tecnología y Telecomunicaciones **EdMIS:** Ministerio de Educación Pública **e-Procurement:** Ministerio de Hacienda **HealthMIS:** Ministerio de Salud **HRMIS:** Dirección General de Servicio Civil **PFMIS:** Ministerio de Hacienda **TaxMIS:** Ministerio de Hacienda
Dominica	**Capabilities:** Caribbean Digital Transformation Project **EdMIS:** Ministry of Education, Human Resource Planning, Vocational Training and National Excellence **e-Procurement:** Government of the Commonwealth of Dominica **HealthMIS:** Dominica Hospitals Authority **HRMIS:** Establishment, Personnel and Training Department **PFMIS:** Government of the Commonwealth of Dominica **TaxMIS:** Government of the Commonwealth of Dominica
Dominican Republic	**HRMIS:** Ministerio de Administración Publica **PFMIS:** Ministerio de Hacienda
Ecuador	**Capabilities:** Ministerio de Telecomunicaciones y de la Sociedad de la Información **EdMIS:** Ministerio de Educación **e-Procurement:** Servicio Nacional de Contratación Pública **HealthMIS:** Ministerio de Salud Pública **HRMIS:** Ministerio del Trabajo **PFMIS:** Ministerio de Economía y Finanzas **TaxMIS:** Servicio de Rentas Internas
Guatemala	**Capabilities:** Comisión Presidencial de Gobierno Abierto y Electrónico **EdMIS:** Ministerio de Educación **e-Procurement:** Ministerio de Finanzas Publicas **HealthMIS:** Ministerio de Salud Pública y Asistencia Social **HRMIS:** Oficina Nacional de Servicio Civil **PFMIS:** Ministerio de Finanzas Publicas **TaxMIS:** Superintendencia de Administración Tributaria
Honduras	**Capabilities:** Oficina de la Presidencia de la República **EdMIS:** Secretaría de Educación **e-Procurement:** Oficina Normativa de Contratación y Adquisiciones del Estado **HealthMIS:** Secretaría de Salud **HRMIS:** Administración Nacional de Servicio Civil **PFMIS:** Secretaría de Finanzas **TaxMIS:** Administración Aduanas
Jamaica	**Capabilities:** eGov Jamaica Limited **e-Procurement:** Public Procurement Commission **HealthMIS:** Ministry of Health and Wellness **TaxMIS:** Tax Administration

(continues on next page)

TABLE A.1 Countries and Organizations That Participated in the Survey *(continued)*

Country	Participating organizations, by questionnaire
Panama	**Capabilities:** Autoridad Nacional para la Innovación Gubernamental **EdMIS:** Ministerio de Educación **e-Procurement:** Dirección General de Contrataciones Públicas **HealthMIS:** Ministerio de Salud **HRMIS:** Ministerio de la Presidencia **PFMIS:** Ministerio de Economía y Finanzas **TaxMIS:** Ministerio de Economía y Finanzas
Paraguay	**Capabilities:** Ministerio de Tecnologías de Información y Comunicación **EdMIS:** Ministerio de Educación y Ciencias **e-Procurement:** Dirección Nacional de Contrataciones Publicas **HealthMIS:** Ministerio de Salud Pública y Bienestar Social **HRMIS:** Viceministerio de Capital Humano y Gestión Organizacional **PFMIS:** Ministerio de Economía y Finanzas **TaxMIS:** Dirección Nacional de Ingresos Tributarios
Peru	**Capabilities:** Secretaría de Gobierno y Transformación Digital **EdMIS:** Ministerio de Educación **PFMIS:** Ministerio de Economía y Finanzas **TaxMIS:** Superintendencia Nacional de Aduanas y de Administración Tributaria
St. Vincent and the Grenadines	**HealthMIS:** Ministry of Health, Wellness and the Environment
Trinidad and Tobago	**Capabilities:** Ministry of Digital Transformation **EdMIS:** Ministry of Education **HealthMIS:** Ministry of Health **HRMIS:** Service Commissions Department **PFMIS:** Ministry of Finance **TaxMIS:** Inland Revenue Division
Uruguay	**Capabilities:** Agencia de Gobierno Electrónico y Sociedad de la Información y del Conocimiento **EdMIS:** Administración Nacional de Educación Pública **e-Procurement:** Agencia Reguladora de Compras Estatales **HealthMIS:** Ministerio de Salud Pública **HRMIS:** Oficina Nacional del Servicio Civil **PFMIS:** Ministerio de Economía y Finanzas **TaxMIS:** Dirección General Impositiva

Source: Original table for this publication.
Note: The table lists the primary organizations involved in completing each questionnaire, but additional organizations also contributed. EdMIS = education management information system; e-Procurement = procurement management information system; HealthMIS = health management information system; HRMIS = human resources management information system; PFMIS = public financial management information system; TaxMIS = tax management information system.

TABLE A.2 Countries That Participated in the Survey, by Questionnaire

Questionnaire	Participating countries
Capabilities	The Bahamas, Belize, Bolivia, Brazil, Chile, Costa Rica, Dominica, Ecuador, Guatemala, Honduras, Jamaica, Panama, Paraguay, Peru, Trinidad and Tobago, Uruguay
EdMIS	Belize, Bolivia, Chile, Costa Rica, Dominica, Ecuador, Guatemala, Honduras, Panama, Paraguay, Peru, Trinidad and Tobago, Uruguay
e-Procurement	Bolivia, Chile, Costa Rica, Dominica, Ecuador, Guatemala, Honduras, Jamaica, Panama, Paraguay, Uruguay
HealthMIS	Belize, Bolivia, Chile, Costa Rica, Dominica, Ecuador, Guatemala, Honduras, Jamaica, Panama, Paraguay, St. Vincent and the Grenadines, Trinidad and Tobago, Uruguay
HRMIS	Barbados, Belize, Bolivia, Chile, Costa Rica, Dominica, Dominican Republic, Ecuador, Guatemala, Honduras, Panama, Paraguay, Trinidad and Tobago, Uruguay
PFMIS	Belize, Bolivia, Brazil, Chile, Colombia, Costa Rica, Dominica, Dominican Republic, Ecuador, Guatemala, Honduras, Panama, Paraguay, Peru, Trinidad and Tobago, Uruguay
TaxMIS	Barbados, Belize, Bolivia, Brazil, Chile, Colombia, Costa Rica, Dominica, Ecuador, Guatemala, Honduras, Jamaica, Panama, Paraguay, Peru, Trinidad and Tobago, Uruguay

Source: Original table for this publication.
Note: The table lists the countries that responded to each questionnaire. EdMIS = education management information system; e-Procurement = procurement management information system; HealthMIS = health management information system; HRMIS = human resources management information system; PFMIS = public financial management information system; TaxMIS = tax management information system.

APPENDIX B

Types of Management Information Systems and Their Functions

Human Resources Management Information System

An HRMIS is a platform designed to streamline and automate the management of human resources within government organizations. It typically covers various human resources functions, such as personnel administration, workforce planning, compensation management, career development and training, attendance tracking, recruitment and deployment, mobility, and performance management (Cortázar Velarde, Lafuente, and Sanginés 2014; Nunberg 2021). The main objectives of an HRMIS are to ensure compliance with existing payroll rules, enhance the productivity of public servants, and ensure efficiency in human resources functions such as recruitment, rotation, and dismissals (Farooq and Kim 2023).

Public Financial Management Information System

A PFMIS is a platform designed to streamline and automate financial operations within budget and treasury units. It typically covers various budget execution functions, such as accounts payable and receivable, commitment and cash management, financial reporting, budget formulation, auditing, debt management, and public investment management. The main objective of a PFMIS is to provide relevant, timely, and reliable financial information to plan, execute, and monitor public finances (Pimenta and Pessoa 2016). Additionally, this type of MIS contributes to the effective and efficient allocation of public resources, fosters fiscal transparency, and links public financial management processes to government functions (Dorotinsky and Watkins 2013; Pimenta and Pessoa 2016).

Procurement Management Information System

An e-Procurement system is a platform designed to streamline the procurement process for government organizations, enhancing the efficiency, competition, and transparency of procurement activities (OECD, n.d.). It typically covers various dimensions of the procurement cycle, such as budget planning and tender preparation; tendering, bidding process, and bid evaluation; contract award and signing; contract execution and monitoring; and logistics (Cocciolo, Samaddar, and Fazekas 2023; UNOPS 2021). The main objective of an e-Procurement system is to enhance transparency, efficiency, and competition by providing key stakeholders with timely, accurate, and accessible procurement information to optimize resource allocation, mitigate risks, and ensure compliance with procurement regulations (World Bank 2011).

Tax Management Information System

A TaxMIS is a platform designed to streamline and automate the management, accounting, and reporting of tax-related tasks and transactions. It typically covers various taxation functions, such as taxpayer registration, return processing, tax payment handling and assessment, management of appeals and objections, tax collection and refunds, registration cancellations, issuance of tax clearance certificates, and cross-institutional reporting (Yoon, Chaithanya, and Kong 2014). The main objectives of a TaxMIS are to provide accurate, reliable tax data to strengthen the core business processes of the tax administration, as well as to control compliance and enhance tax collection enforcement mechanisms (Junquera-Varela and Lucas-Mas 2024).

Education Management Information System

An EdMIS is a platform that enables the public sector to collect, monitor, manage, analyze, and disseminate information about educational inputs, processes, and outcomes (Abdul-Hamid 2017). It typically covers various educational planning, monitoring, and evaluation processes, including student enrollment, attendance tracking, academic performance analysis, curriculum management, teacher deployment, facilities and materials management, financial resource management, and school infrastructure maintenance (Abdul-Hamid 2017). The main objective of an EdMIS is to provide systematic, relevant, timely, and accurate information to enable governments to examine and strengthen the performance of their education systems (Porta and Arcia 2011).

Health Management Information System

A HealthMIS is a platform designed to streamline and automate the management and delivery of health care services within public health systems. It typically covers various dimensions of the health care system, including individual patient records, disease surveillance, services delivered, health outcomes, health care utilization patterns, health facility management, community-level records, pharmaceutical inventory, and health personnel management (Lippeveld et al. 2019). The main objectives of a HealthMIS are to generate information at all levels of the health system to enhance health service delivery and optimally allocate resources (PAHO 2021).

REFERENCES

Abdul-Hamid, Husein. 2017. "What Is an Education Management Information System and Who Uses It?" In *Data for Learning: Building a Smart Education Data System*, 7–16. Washington, DC: World Bank. https://doi.org/10.1596/978-1-4648-1099-2.

Cocciolo, Serena, Suxhmita Samaddar, and Mihaly Fazekas. 2023. "Government Analytics Using Procurement Data." In *The Government Analytics Handbook: Leveraging Data to Strengthen Public Administration*, edited by Daniel Rogger and Christian Schuster, chap. 12. Washington, DC: World Bank. https://doi.org/10.1596/978-1-4648-1957-5.

Cortázar Velarde, Juan Carlos, Mariano Lafuente, and Mario Sanginés, eds. 2014. *Serving Citizens: A Decade of Civil Service Reforms in Latin America (2004–13)*. Washington, DC: Inter-American Development Bank. https://publications.iadb.org/en/serving-citizens-decade-civil-service-reforms-latin-america-2004-13.

Dorotinsky, William, and Joanna Watkins. 2013. "Government Financial Management Information Systems." In *The International Handbook of Public Financial Management*, edited by Richard Allen, Richard Hemming, and Barry H. Potter, chap. 36. New York: Palgrave Macmillan. https://doi.org/10.1057/9781137315304_37.

Farooq, Khuram, and Galileu Kim. 2023. "Creating Data Infrastructures for Government Analytics." In *The Government Analytics Handbook: Leveraging Data to Strengthen Public Administration*, edited by Daniel Rogger and Christian Schuster, chap. 9. Washington, DC: World Bank. https://doi.org/10.1596/978-1-4648-1957-5.

Junquera-Varela, Raúl Félix, and Cristian Óliver Lucas-Mas, eds. 2024. *Revenue Administration Handbook*. Washington, DC: World Bank. https://doi.org/10.1596/978-1-4648-2053-3.

Lippeveld, Theo, Tariq Azim, David Boone, Vikas Dwivedi, Michael Edwards, and Carla AbouZahr. 2019. "Health Management Information Systems: Backbone of the Health System." In *The Palgrave Handbook of Global Health Data Methods for Policy and Practice*, edited by Sarah B. Macfarlane and Carla AbouZahr, 165–81. London: Palgrave Macmillan. https://doi.org/10.1057/978-1-137-54984-6_9.

Nunberg, Barbara. 2021. "Strengthening Subnational Human Resource Management Systems: A Primer. Equitable Growth, Finance and Institutions Insight." World Bank, Washington, DC. https://documents.worldbank.org/pt/publication/documents-reports/documentdetail/099225502022348809/p1754490dbaaa300f0a2b60af27d2e3508c.

OECD (Organisation for Economic Co-operation and Development). n.d. "Methodology for Assessing Procurement Systems." Accessed March 30, 2024. https://www.oecd.org/gov/public-procurement/methodology-assessing-procurement/.

PAHO (Pan American Health Organization). 2021. *Eight Guiding Principles of Digital Transformation of the Health Sector: A Call to Pan American Action*. Washington, DC: PAHO. https://iris.paho.org/handle/10665.2/54256.

Pimenta, Carlos, and Mario Pessoa, eds. 2016. *Public Financial Management in Latin America: The Key to Efficiency and Transparency*. Washington, DC: International Monetary Fund. https://doi.org/10.18235/0000083.

Porta, Emilio, and Gustavo Arcia. 2011. "Improving Information Systems for Planning and Policy Dialogue: The SABER EMIS Assessment Tool." World Bank, Washington, DC. https://www.academia.edu/41964853/Improving_Information_Systems_for_Planning_and_Policy_Dialogue_The_SABER_EMIS_Assessment_Tool_SABER_System_Assessment_and_Benchmarking_for_Education_Results.

UNOPS (United Nations Office for Project Services). 2021. *UNOPS Procurement Manual*. Revision 7, last modified July 1, 2021. Copenhagen, Denmark: UNOPS. https://content.unops.org/service-Line-Documents/Procurement/UNOPS-Procurement-Manual-2021_EN.pdf.

World Bank. 2011. *e-Procurement Reference Guide*. Washington, DC: World Bank. https://documents1.worldbank.org/curated/ar/751741468163749785/pdf/882160WP0Box380ementReferenceGuide.pdf.

Yoon, Seok Yong, Chava Chaithanya, and Dongsung Kong. 2014. *Tool Kit for Tax Administration Management Information System*. Mandaluyong, Philippines: Asian Development Bank. https://www.adb.org/sites/default/files/publication/150133/tool-kit-tax-administration-management-information-system.pdf.